Children's Intellectual Rights

David Moshman, *Editor*
University of Nebraska–Lincoln

NEW DIRECTIONS FOR CHILD DEVELOPMENT
WILLIAM DAMON, *Editor-in-Chief*
Clark University

Number 33, Fall 1986

Paperback sourcebooks in
The Jossey-Bass Social and Behavioral Sciences Series

Jossey-Bass Inc., Publishers
San Francisco • London

David Moshman (ed.).
Children's Intellectual Rights.
New Directions for Child Development, no. 33.
San Francisco: Jossey-Bass, 1986.

New Directions for Child Development
William Damon, *Editor-in-Chief*

Copyright © 1986 by Jossey-Bass Inc., Publishers
and
Jossey-Bass Limited

Copyright under International, Pan American, and Universal
Copyright Conventions. All rights reserved. No part of
this issue may be reproduced in any form—except for brief
quotation (not to exceed 500 words) in a review or professional
work—without permission in writing from the publishers.

New Directions for Child Development (publication number USPS
494-090) is published quarterly by Jossey-Bass Inc., Publishers.
Second-class postage paid at San Francisco, California, and at
additional mailing offices. POSTMASTER: Send address changes to
Jossey-Bass Inc., Publishers, 433 California Street, San Francisco,
California 94104.

Editorial correspondence should be sent to the Editor-in-Chief,
William Damon, Department of Psychology, Clark University,
Worcester, Massachusetts 01610.

Library of Congress Catalog Card Number 85-644581

International Standard Serial Number ISSN 0195-2269

International Standard Book Number ISBN 1-55542-996-3

Cover art by WILLI BAUM

Manufactured in the United States of America

Ordering Information

The paperback sourcebooks listed below are published quarterly and can be ordered either by subscription or single-copy.

Subscriptions cost $40.00 per year for institutions, agencies, and libraries. Individuals can subscribe at the special rate of $30.00 per year *if payment is by personal check*. (Note that the full rate of $40.00 applies if payment is by institutional check, even if the subscription is designated for an individual.) Standing orders are accepted.

Single copies are available at $9.95 when payment accompanies order, and *all single-copy orders under $25.00 must include payment*. (California, New Jersey, New York, and Washington, D.C., residents please include appropriate sales tax.) For billed orders, cost per copy is $9.95 plus postage and handling. (Prices subject to change without notice.)

Bulk orders (ten or more copies) of any individual sourcebook are available at the following discounted prices: 10-49 copies, $8.95 each; 50-100 copies, $7.96 each; over 100 copies, *inquire*. Sales tax and postage and handling charges apply as for single copy orders.

Please note that these prices are for the academic year 1986-1987 and are subject to change without prior notice. Also, some titles may be out of print and therefore not available for use.

To ensure correct and prompt delivery, all orders must give either the *name of an individual* or an *official purchase order number*. Please submit your order as follows:

> *Subscriptions:* specify series and year subscription is to begin.
> *Single Copies:* specify sourcebook code (such as, CD1) and first two words of title.

> Mail orders for United States and Possessions, Latin America, Canada, Japan, Australia, and New Zealand to:
> Jossey-Bass Inc., Publishers
> 433 California Street
> San Francisco, California 94104

> Mail orders for all other parts of the world to:
> Jossey-Bass Limited
> 28 Banner Street
> London EC1Y 8QE

New Directions for Child Development Series
William Damon, *Editor-in-Chief*

CD1 *Social Cognition,* William Damon
CD2 *Moral Development,* William Damon
CD3 *Early Symbolization,* Howard Gardner, Dennie Wolf

CD4	*Social Interaction and Communication During Infancy,* Ina C. Uzgiris
CD5	*Intellectual Development Beyond Childhood,* Deanna Kuhn
CD6	*Fact, Fiction, and Fantasy in Childhood,* Ellen Winner, Howard Gardner
CD7	*Clinical-Developmental Psychology,* Robert L. Selman, Regina Yando
CD8	*Anthropological Perspectives on Child Development,* Charles M. Super, Sara Harkness
CD9	*Children's Play,* Kenneth H. Rubin
CD10	*Children's Memory,* Marion Perlmutter
CD11	*Developmental Perspectives on Child Maltreatment,* Ross Rizley, Dante Cicchetti
CD12	*Cognitive Development,* Kurt W. Fischer
CD13	*Viewing Children Through Television,* Hope Kelly, Howard Gardner
CD14	*Childrens' Conceptions of Health, Illness, and Bodily Functions,* Roger Bibace, Mary E. Walsh
CD15	*Children's Conceptions of Spatial Relationships,* Robert Cohen
CD16	*Emotional Development,* Dante Cicchetti, Petra Hesse
CD17	*Developmental Approaches to Giftedness and Creativity,* David Henry Feldman
CD18	*Children's Planning Strategies,* David Forbes, Mark T. Greenberg
CD19	*Children and Divorce,* Lawrence A. Kurdek
CD20	*Child Development and International Development: Research-Policy Interfaces,* Daniel A. Wagner
CD21	*Levels and Transitions in Children's Development,* Kurt W. Fischer
CD22	*Adolescent Development in the Family,* Harold D. Grotevant, Catherine R. Cooper
CD23	*Children's Learning in the "Zone of Proximal Development,"* Barbara Rogoff, James V. Wertsch
CD24	*Children in Families Under Stress,* Anna-Beth Doyle, Dolores Gold, Debbie S. Moscowitz
CD25	*Analyzing Children's Play Dialogues,* Frank Kessel, Artin Göncû
CD26	*Childhood Depression,* Dante Cicchetti, Karen Schneider-Rosen
CD27	*The Development of Reading Skills,* Thomas H. Carr
CD28	*Children and Computers,* Elisa L. Klein
CD29	*Peer Conflict and Psychological Growth,* Marvin W. Berkowitz
CD30	*Identity in Adolescence: Processes and Contents,* Alan S. Waterman
CD31	*Temperament and Social Interaction,* Jacqueline V. Lerner, Richard M. Lerner
CD32	*Early Experience and the Development of Competence,* William Fowler

Contents

Editor's Notes 1
David Moshman

1. The Constitution and the Child's Right to 7
Freedom from Political Indoctrination
Tyll van Geel
Does the Constitution permit government indoctrination of children? Does it permit indoctrination by parents?

2. Children's Intellectual Rights: A First Amendment 25
Analysis
David Moshman
Should children be distinguished from adults with respect to freedoms of religion and expression?

3. Critical Thinking as an Intellectual Right 39
Harvey Siegel
What is wrong with indoctrination? What *should* be the goal of education?

4. Three Children's Rights Claims and Some Reservations 51
Colin Wringe
Do children's intellectual rights extend to the point of allowing them to harm themselves or others?

5. Populism, School Prayer, and the Courts: 63
Confessions of an Expert Witness
Gary B. Melton
If a deeply committed majority votes for prayer in the public schools, will they have their way? Should they?

6. Children's Intellectual Rights: Implications for 75
Educational Policy
Bridget A. Franks
Given the political realities of public schools, is protection of student rights really feasible?

Index 89

Editor's Notes

The last decade has seen an explosion of political controversy over the education of children. Many of the questions raised have direct implications for parent-child relations as well. An overview of these questions illustrates the sensitivity, complexity, and broad significance of the issues.

Who should decide what children see, hear, and read? Do they have a right to read books, listen to music, or see movies adults disapprove of? Is it proper to remove a book from a school library or curriculum because of its political views? Is it proper to remove a book because it shows women in nontraditional roles? Because it shows women in traditional roles? Because it has a religious theme? Because it has an antireligious theme? Because it is racist? Because it presents a point of view (such as evolution) some religions disapprove of? Because it presents a point of view (such as "scientific" creationism) scientists disagree with?

What about children's own expression? Should there be limits on what they are allowed to say? On what they are allowed to write? On what they publish in student newspapers? Should they be permitted to criticize the government, their schools, their teachers, their parents, or their peers? Should there be any limits on this?

Do children have a right to hold, express, and act on their own religious beliefs? Should they be permitted to pray in school? Should they be allowed to meet in school facilities for religious activities? Should schools be required, permitted, or forbidden to set aside time and facilities for religious activities?

May adults inculcate ideas or values in their dealings with children? Should they do so? May adults require children to believe or express certain things? Should schools be value-neutral? Can they be? Should we draw a line between inculcation and indoctrination? Can this be done?

Do children have a right to learn? To develop? To be educated? Should education be compulsory? What if a child doesn't want to be educated? What if a parent doesn't want his or her child educated? If education is compulsory, who decides what counts as education? Is education the learning of facts? Does it include values? Does it include the development of critical thinking?

Are we justified in distinguishing children from adults for the purpose of according or restricting rights? Should children have special privileges (such as a right to free education) simply because they are children? Should children be subject to special limitations (such as restrictions on free expression) simply because they are children? Is the child's age a relevant consideration?

All the above questions relate to children's intellectual rights. We may define intellectual rights as including the right to use and develop one's intellect, including access to information and ideas, freedom to believe what one chooses, freedom to express one's beliefs, and, perhaps, freedom to act on those beliefs. The general question of intellectual rights, then, is a question of whether and to what extent people have (or should have) these sorts of rights. The specific question addressed in this volume is whether and to what extent such rights apply to children.

The issue of children's intellectual rights is in part a legal matter. For example, what intellectual rights do American children have under the laws of the United States and the various state governments? What intellectual rights, if any, are they guaranteed under the U.S. Constitution and the various state constitutions? In the numerous legal battles over children's intellectual rights, what interpretations have been made by the courts?

Legal analysis, however, does not exhaust the issue. Even if children had no legal rights whatsoever, one could still argue that they are entitled to something—that is, that they have moral, ethical, or "natural" rights. In fact, a major rationale for giving children legal protection is to prevent them from being treated improperly or unjustly; this rationale implies that treating children in certain ways would be ethically wrong even if it were not against the law. Thus, one can argue that the law simply gives legal status to the rights children already have. But what are those broader, extralegal rights, and how can one justify them? This is a question not of law but of ethics or, more broadly, of philosophy.

It appears, then, that we can distinguish two senses of children's intellectual rights—legal rights, which are a matter of law, and ethical rights, which are a matter of philosophy. In addressing rights from either perspective, however, one immediately runs into questions about the nature of children. Should sixteen-year-olds have the same rights as adults? What about ten-year-olds? What about four-year-olds? The answers seem to depend on what characteristics we see as the legal or ethical bases for adult rights and whether children at various ages have those characteristics. But what children are like at various ages is an empirical question and cannot be answered by scrutiny of the Constitution or by conceptual analysis of ethical theories. It can be answered only by empirical evidence about children—that is, through psychological research. Consideration of children's intellectual rights raises empirical questions about children's intellects and thus brings us into the domains of cognitive and developmental psychology.

Finally, although children's intellectual rights can be discussed at an abstract level, it is usually in the context of schools that the issue comes up. People of many different political views recognize that schools have a powerful impact on the minds of the next generation and are justifiably concerned about the nature of this impact. An important perspective on schools is to consider what intellectual rights students have and to what extent those rights are respected by teachers, administrators, school boards, and legislatures. Thus, in addition to the legal, philosophical, and psychological considerations, children's intellectual rights are—or should be—a central issue of educational policy.

With the above considerations in mind, the authors of this volume were selected to give broad representation to legal, philosophical, psychological, and educational perspectives on children's intellectual rights. Each is interdisciplinary in his or her own work, representing at least two of the above disciplines. The six together give this volume strong representation from all four fields.

In the first chapter, Tyll van Geel analyzes the political indoctrination of children from a legal point of view. He considers the traditional interpretation, accepted in many court decisions, that there are no constitutional limits on indoctrination, and he explores an alternative, in which the Constitution is construed as forbidding indoctrination by parents and by public schools. Van Geel ultimately rejects both approaches and argues for a compromise interpretation, in which the Constitution is seen as forbidding public schools, as agents of government, from indoctrinating children, while setting no limits on parents.

In the second chapter, David Moshman proposes six legal principles of children's intellectual rights that, he argues, can be derived from the First Amendment. These principles essentially accord children the same intellectual rights as adults, except when relevant differences can be empirically demonstrated on the basis of psychological research. In accord with van Geel's analysis, Moshman argues that only the government (including public schools) is constitutionally obligated to act in accord with these principles. He proposes, however, that the principles can serve as ethical guidelines for parents and private schools as well.

Although Moshman suggests that at least some intellectual rights of children can be morally justified, he does not provide such justification. This is a task taken up in the third chapter by Harvey Siegel, who provides a philosophical defense of the view that children have an ethical right to the sort of education that will help them become critical thinkers. His argument is based on the Kantian principle of respect for persons and on the role of critical thinking in the development of self-sufficiency, initiation into rational traditions, and preparation for democratic citizenship. Corresponding to van Geel's and Moshman's legal arguments against indoctrination by government, Siegel's more general philosophical approach argues for a child's right not to be indoctrinated by *anyone*. In connection with this, he articulates and defends an important distinction between (morally repugnant) indoctrination and nonindoctrinative inculcation of beliefs and attitudes.

Continuing in a philosophical vein, Colin Wringe, in the fourth chapter, considers whether children have a right to education, to access to knowledge, and to freedom of expression. Although sympathetic to Siegel's view that children should be seen as persons with broad intellectual rights, Wringe explores some difficult concrete cases that test the limits of those rights. How much education is every child entitled to, and who is obliged to provide that education? Can children be harmed by unlimited access to information, and are adults thus justified in protecting them? Should children be permitted to express anything whatsoever, regardless of its effects on their parents, teachers, or schoolmates? Wringe's thoughtful analyses illustrate the importance and difficulty of applying abstract principles to concrete situations.

The last two contributions pursue the issue of application. In the fifth chapter, Gary B. Melton provides an insider's account of a specific court case, involving prayer in public schools, in which he served as an expert witness. We see here the interrelations of many levels of analysis, covering the general constitutional issue of separation of church and state, the more specific issue of school prayer, the particular West Virginia law under legal challenge, and the perceptions of a Catholic boy and a Jewish girl directly affected. Melton's testimony, summarized in his chapter, focused on children's conceptions of prayer, their understanding of rights, their susceptibility to both peer and adult pressure, and their likely reactions to tolerance and intolerance. The chapter provides a clear example of how psychological evidence about children can be brought to bear in resolving a legal issue.

In the concluding chapter, Bridget A. Franks assesses the status of children's intellectual rights in educational policy. She examines the history, nature, and purpose of public schools, detailing a complex interaction of rights, interests, functions, and constraints. Considering the intellectual rights of students from the perspectives of educators, parents, and the students themselves, she includes specific practical guidelines for each of these three groups. Franks demonstrates that abstract principles of children's intellectual rights will not get us very far if we are naive about the complex realities and practicalities of public schools. Nevertheless, she argues, we are sure to lose our way in these very complexities unless we recognize and are committed to student rights.

The issue of children's intellectual rights is both a fascinating multidisciplinary challenge and a matter of great practical importance. The authors and I hope the present volume will inspire further work on this topic, and we believe efforts of this sort can have a positive impact on the intellectual lives of children.

David Moshman
Editor

David Moshman is associate professor of educational psychology at the University of Nebraska–Lincoln and first vice-president of the Nebraska Civil Liberties Union. His primary research interests are the intellectual rights of children and students and the development of reasoning during adolescence and beyond.

Source: From LIFE IS HELL, by Matt Groening. Copyright © 1984, 1985 by Matt Groening. Reprinted by permission of Pantheon Books, a division of Random House, Inc.

Although the Constitution can and should be interpreted to protect children from political indoctrination by government, it may not and should not be interpreted to protect children from political indoctrination by their parents.

The Constitution and the Child's Right to Freedom from Political Indoctrination

Tyll van Geel

Does the Supreme Court's interpretation of the Constitution protect children from "educational" efforts intended to get them to believe in political propositions so that nothing will subsequently shake that belief? If not, *should* the Constitution be interpreted to protect the child against political indoctrination, that is, should the Constitution be read as recognizing a child's right to self-determination in the formation of political beliefs? To begin answering these questions it is important to note that the questions as stated do not draw a distinction between a right held by a child vis-à-vis the government and/or a child vis-à-vis his or her parents. This distinction will be refined in the following discussion of four models of the child-parent-state relationship.

Under the Traditional Model, the child enjoys no right not to be indoctrinated by either parents or government operating through a public school system—a system that parents are legally free to reject in favor of private schooling. Two important traditions lie at the heart of this model: respect for parental authority to control the upbringing of the child, and respect for the authority of public schools to seek to inculcate students politically. (It is well settled that public schools constitutionally may not attempt religious inculcation; this topic will not be discussed in this chapter. The precise difference between religious and political inculcation is, of course, itself a difficult question also not taken up.)

The two traditions of the Traditional Model are supported by categorically different kinds of reasons. The autonomy of the family unit and the authority of the parent are accepted as "natural rights," which predate the positive law of the states, and which have been implicitly recognized by the Constitution. As for the authority of the states to inculcate public school pupils, this rests not on a notion of natural rights but on the prudential claim that states should exercise their police and *parens partriae* powers to inculcate children with those values thought necessary to make them into good citizens and necessary for maintaining a stable democratic form of government. An inevitable consequence of this model is that a particular child may be subjected to conflicting inculcation efforts by parents and public schools.

The second model I call the Platonic Model, after the vision of a utopia developed by Plato in his dialogue *The Republic*. Under this conception of the child-parent-state relationship, one way or another it is the state that takes over the task of determining how the child should be indoctrinated. The least extreme version of this model would involve state inculcation in the public schools, and state regulation of private education to ensure that students are properly inculcated. Under a different version, parents would be required to send their children to public institutions, where they would be inculcated under state direction. The most extreme version of this model would have children enrolled in residential schools to ensure that parents had little or no opportunity to undertake their own private programs of inculcation.

The model I have called the Open Future Model stands in dramatic contrast to the first two. (The name is taken from Feinberg, 1980.) Under this model, the child would enjoy a right to be free from the efforts of both parents and government to instill unshakeable political beliefs. The educational program provided by parents and government would seek to assure the child of having the option and the freedom, as an adult, of taking a political direction of his or her own choosing. Thus, the model would require that each child's natural capacity for independent political self-determination would be fostered, and not subjected to a program designed to frustrate or enfeeble that capacity. The aim must be that, upon reaching adulthood, the individual's political beliefs and opinions may fairly be said to be his or hers, and not the product of an effective program of inculcation.

The Open Future Model has both a tough and a weak version. In the tough version, the child must be educated so that he or she enters adulthood with both a developed capacity for critical rationality and an open mind on political issues (Richards, 1980, p. 22). In the weak version, the educational program would also be expected to develop the child's capacity for critical rationality, but parents and/or government would be permitted to try to get the child to accept their preferred political propositions, so long as the aim were merely to get the child to hold to the propositions as working hypotheses, or rebuttable presumptions. Thus, the child might grow into an autonomous adulthood, holding to certain beliefs, but would have the capacity to question those beliefs; that is, those beliefs would not be so fixed as to be incapable of being dislodged and/or modified by critical analysis. As a practical matter, the kind of educational program required in this case would develop and respect the child's capacity to assess what adult educators say. Children would be provided with diverse and stimulating education and encouraged to ask questions. Although parents and public schools might espouse their own political values and principles, they would be expected to indicate to the child that there might be disagreement over these matters. Educators would also be required to respond to the child's questions in a way that showed respect for the child's developing capacity for critical rationality and respect for the child's expression of dissenting opinion (Richards, 1980, pp. 25, 27; McLauglin, 1984, p. 81).

The fourth model I have termed the Asymmetrical Model, because it treats the authority of parents to inculcate, and the authority of the public schools to inculcate, differently. That is, parents would be permitted to seek to inculcate their own beliefs and values, but the public schools would be prohibited from deliberate indoctrination. The program of the public schools would have to be like the one described in connection with the Open Future Model.

The two questions posed at the outset of this chapter now need to be refined: Which of the four models does the Supreme Court embrace as the correct interpretation of the Constitution? And which of the four models *should* the Court embrace as the correct interpretation of the Constitution? In the first section of this chapter, I shall argue that Supreme Court precedent embraces the Traditional Model. The second section briefly deals with the Platonic Model. In the third section, I shall offer an alternative interpretation of the Constitution that supports the Open Future Model. In this section, I shall also deal with the Platonic Model. In the last section, I shall argue that neither the Traditional Model nor the Open Future Model represents the best interpretation of the Constitution; I shall argue instead that the Asymmetrical Model should be the preferred interpretation of the Constitution. Essential to the making of this argument is adoption of a particular approach to constitutional interpretation, an approach different from those that tend to support the Traditional and Open Future

Models. Thus, the last section will discuss three alternative approaches to constitutional interpretation.

Supreme Court Precedent and the Traditional Model

In a variety of opinions, the Supreme Court has embraced the twin pillars of the Traditional Model, the authority of parents and of public schools to shape the beliefs and viewpoints of children. In a decision precluding the state of Oregon from eliminating the option of parents to send their children to private schools, the Court said (*Pierce* v. *Society of Sisters*, 1925, p. 534) that the state law "unreasonably interferes with the liberty of parents and guardians to direct the upbringing and education of children under their control." In *Meyer* v. *Nebraska* (1923, p. 401) the Court, in striking down a law regulating the teaching of foreign languages to children, said the law interfered with "the power of parents to control the education of their own." In *Wisconsin* v. *Yoder* (1972, p. 233) the Court, in upholding the right of Amish parents to exempt their children from the last two years of required formal education, said, "However read, the Court's decision in *Pierce* stands as a charter of the rights of parents to direct the religious upbringing of their children." In a subsequent case, the Court reinforced the theme that parents enjoy substantial control even over the nonreligious education of their children. Thus, the Court wrote (*Parham* v. *J.R.*, 1979, pp. 603–604), "We cannot assume that the result in *Meyer* v. *Nebraska* . . . and *Pierce* v. *Society of Sisters* . . . would have been different if the children there had announced a preference to learn only English or a preference to go to a public, rather than a church, school." And in *Runyon* v. *McCrary* (1976), the Court said in dictum that it may be assumed the First Amendment protects the right of parents to send their children to schools that promote a belief in racial segregation. Nevertheless, there is little doubt that the state may prohibit instruction intended to incite and prepare students for lawless action now, if circumstances are such as reasonably to justify apprehension such action will occur (*Yates* v. *United States*, 1957).

In sum, the Court, by acknowledging the authority of parents to control the upbringing of their children, has said two things: First, children do not enjoy a constitutional right vis-à-vis their parents not to be inculcated by them. Hence, the state neither has the legal duty to protect children vis-à-vis their parents' efforts to inculcate, nor has it the authority to take steps against a parent in the name of a child who seeks to be freed of his or her parents' program of inculcation. Second, parental rights vis-à-vis the state bar the state from forcing parents for its own reasons (for example, its concept of a good education or its concept of what morality demands) to provide their children with an education that preserves the children's intellectual options. This last point is perhaps most strongly recognized in *Wisconsin* v. *Yoder* (1972), in which the Court permitted the Amish parents to isolate their children on family farms and provide education intended to ensure that the children would remain within and part of the Amish community (Feinberg, 1980). Thus, it appears the Court would prohibit a state's requiring private schools to eschew indoctrination and embrace, for example, a program of instruction designed to promote critical thinking.

I turn now to the second pillar of the Traditional Model. The Supreme Court's support of the authority of the public schools to inculcate pupils has been, if anything, more explicit. Every Justice on the current Supreme Court has embraced the proposition that "public schools are vitally important [as] vehicles for inculcating fundamental values necessary to the maintenance of a democratic political system. . . . We are therefore in full agreement . . . that local school boards must be permitted 'to establish and apply their curriculum in such a way as to transmit community values,' and that 'there is a legitimate and substantial community interest in promoting respect for authority and traditional values, be they social, moral, or political.'" (*Board of Education* v. *Pico*, 1982, pp. 864, 876, 889, 913-914; *Ambach* v. *Norwick*, 1979, pp. 76-77; *Plyler* v. *Doe*, 1982, p. 221).

In sum, there is ample evidence that the Supreme Court has adopted the Traditional Model as the correct interpretation of the Constitution. This is politically the easiest position for the Court to take, since it does the least to disturb existing practices. This interpretation of the Constitution avoids the wrath of those "strict constructionists" who would argue that any other interpretation would take the meaning of the Constitution beyond what the original framers intended. But assuming the Court had adopted the Traditional Model, we still can ask whether this model is the best one to use. It is to this question that I now turn.

The Platonic Model

Before turning to the case for the Open Future Model, I want briefly to dispose of the Platonic Model. The significant difference between this model and the Traditional Model is the way the state intrudes upon the parent's role in inculcating the child. Thus, the central and unique question raised by this model is the issue of the right of the parent vis-à-vis the state to control the upbringing of the child. I will keep my comments on this model brief, because the central focus of this chapter is on the intellectual rights of the child, and this question is treated in conjunction with the other models. Also recall that I have already noted, in connection with the discussion of the Traditional Model, that the Supreme Court has strongly protected the rights of parents to control the upbringing of their children. Let me just add that the Supreme Court has in dictum explicitly rejected the more extreme versions of this model when it wrote (*Meyer* v.

Nebraska, 1923, pp. 401-402) that Plato's vision of a state in which the offspring of parents were removed from their homes to be educated by the state rested on ideas "wholly different from those upon which our institutions rest."

The Open Future Model and the Constitution

There are reasons to believe that the Open Future Model is a plausible interpretation of the Constitution and preferable both to the traditional Model and to the Platonic Model. I will outline the case for this model in two basic steps: First, I will develop the argument that public schools ought to be constitutionally prohibited from attempting to inculcate pupils. Second, I will extend this argument to parents.

I begin the argument on behalf of the Open Future Model by noting that in a number of cases the Supreme Court has expressly and strongly protected the right of the individual to choose his or her own beliefs. In the context of an establishment-clause case, the Court wrote (*Wallace* v. *Jaffree,* 1985, p. 39) that freedom of conscience is "the central liberty that unifies the various clauses of the First Amendment." Continuing, the Court noted (p. 40), "Just as the right to speak and the right to refrain from speaking are complementary components of a broader concept of individual freedom of mind, so also the individual's freedom to choose his own creed is the counterpart of his right to refrain from accepting the creed established by the majority." The Court has also written (*West Virginia State Board of Education* v. *Barnette,* 1943, p. 642), that "no official, high or petty, can prescribe what shall be orthodox in politics, nationalism, religion, or other matters of opinion." Indeed, in other contexts the Court has prohibited the criminal punishment of individuals merely because of the beliefs they hold (*Scales* v. *United States,* 1961, pp. 209, 220; *American Communications Association* v. *Douds,* 1950, p. 408; *Reynolds* v. *United States,* 1878, p. 166). Government's denying benefits to individuals because of beliefs held has also been prohibited (*Branti* v. *Finkel,* 1980; *Elrod* v. *Burns,* 1976; *Keyishian* v. *Board of Regents,* 1967; *Sherbert* v. *Verner,* 1963).

There are good reasons for the Court to have taken this unyielding stand in protecting the self-determination of belief (van Geel, 1983). Whatever definition of democracy one may embrace, at the heart of the notion of democracy is the principle that public opinion should control government, and not the other way around. To speak of a government that rests on the consent of the governed when that consent has been manufactured by the government is to echo the kinds of slogans used by the Party in Orwell's *1984:* "War is Peace." The importance the Constitution attaches to the protection of the right to freedom of expression would make little sense if the thoughts expressed were not self-determined but rather the product of political indoctrination. As Emerson (1970, pp. 21-22) puts it:

> Belief . . . is not strictly "expression." Forming or holding a belief occurs prior to expression. But it is the first stage in the process of expression, and it tends to progress into expression. Hence, safeguarding the right to form and hold beliefs is essential in maintaining a system of freedom of expression. Freedom of belief, therefore, must be held included within the protection of the First Amendment. This proposition has indeed been accepted consistently and without hesitation by all courts and commentators.

Democratic theory requires that citizens be permitted to entertain the possibility of changing their form of government, and a system of indoctrination that seriously seeks to preclude this possibility must be viewed as inconsistent with democratic theory itself. Furthermore, prohibiting governmental inculcation is a necessary prophylactic, since we cannot be sure that, given the nature of the political process, if government had the authority to inculcate it would choose to inculcate beliefs and values that were morally acceptable or not otherwise in error. If people are to be held legally and morally responsible for actions caused by their political beliefs, those beliefs must be self-determined. To attempt to inculcate in the young a fixed set of beliefs is to impede their ability to adapt to a changing society and world and to interfere with their political "immunization systems," which they may need to protect themselves against the siren song of a charismatic political figure who, evoking the platitudes in which the public has been indoctrinated, seeks to lead the nation in an ultimately self-destructive direction.

The advocate for the authority of public schools to inculcate pupils may respond by admitting, for the sake of argument, that public school students have a right not to be indoctrinated, yet may also argue that no right is absolute and that government may have a compelling set of reasons for overriding a right. For example, it may be argued that governmental indoctrination is needed to maintain a stable and democratic government, that it is needed to establish consensus to reduce politically inspired violence, and that it is necessary to produce a loyal and patriotic citizenry. The central difficulty with this line of argument is that there is no convincing empirical base to support these claims (van Geel, 1983, pp. 262-289), and without empirical support these arguments are insufficient to provide warrant for the invasion of what must be viewed as a fundamental constitutional right. The argument thus concludes that government may not seek to inculcate youth in political beliefs and thereby infringe on the right of self-determination of political beliefs.

The argument in support of the Open Future Model cannot be complete until an argument has also been mounted to support the claim that parents, like the public schools, may not seek to interfere with children's right to self-determination of political beliefs. This is clearly the most difficult part of the general argument for the Open Future Model, since it requires that a case be made for the proposition that the Constitution should govern the relationship between two private citizens—parent and child—when, by its own express terms, the Constitution directly addresses only what government may or may not do. (The First Amendment states, "Congress shall make no law respecting an establishment of religion, or prohibiting the free exercise thereof; or abridging the freedom of speech, or of the press; or the right of the people peaceably to assemble, and to petition the Government for a redress of grievances.") There are two basic ways in which to overcome this difficulty. One may either establish that the parent is in some sense a "state actor" and that the Constitution directly controls the parent's actions in the same way it controls the actions of public school officials, or one may attempt to establish that the Constitution imposes on the state the affirmative duty to protect the child against parents who seek to indoctrinate. I shall explore both lines of argument.

The "state actor" argument is best approached by a brief statement of its main points: First, for the reasons noted above, children have a constitutional right not to be indoctrinated. Second, parents, for reasons to be explored in a moment, must be deemed "state actors." Hence, when parents seek to inculcate their children, they stand in the same position vis-à-vis the children as the public schools, and the children, or a state agency acting as guardian, may invoke in the courts the protection of the Constitution to enjoin the parents from continuing. Since the first point in this argument has been addressed earlier, the obviously crucial point to be established is the claim that parents are "state actors."

There are three ways this latter point might be supported. (1) It can be argued, contrary to the assumption of the Traditional Model, that the authority of parents to inculcate their children is not a "natural right" recognized by the Constitution but is purely a product of state positive law. In other words, when parents exert authority over their children to inculcate them, they are evoking an authority they would not otherwise have, but for the state having adopted state law, which permits such inculcation (compare *Terry* v. *Adams*, 1953; *Nixon* v. *Condon*, 1932). Thus, when parents act to inculcate their children, they are in effect acting on behalf of the state. (2) It could also be argued that "state action" is involved because of the state's willingness to stand ready to enforce the parents' authority against the child (compare *Shelly* v. *Kramer*, 1948). (3) Parents, in educating children, are exercising a "public function"; hence, like government, they must be subject to the restrictions of the Constitution (compare *March* v. *Alabama*, 1946; *Terry* v. *Adams*, 1953).

Although these plausible arguments are based on Supreme Court precedent, it is unlikely that today's Supreme Court would embrace any of them. First, the Court has accepted the view that parental rights are rooted in something other than positive state law (*Pierce* v. *Society of Sisters,* 1925). Second, the Court today holds the position that the Constitution applies by its own force directly to private actors only if the state has exercised coercive power or has provided significant encouragement, so that the choice of the private actor may be deemed to be that of the state (*Blum* v. *Yaretsky, 1982; Flagg Bros. Inc.* v. *Brooks,* 1978). Finally, the "public function" doctrine, as interpreted by today's Court, applies only if the private actor carried out a function that had traditionally been exclusively reserved to the state (*Jackson* v. *Metropolitan Edison Co.,* 1974). It is thus necessary to turn to another argument, which does not rest on the assumption that the parent is a "state actor." The gist of this argument is that, even assuming parents have a constitutional right to control the upbringing of their children, and even assuming they are not "state actors," a system of state law that permits parents to infringe on the right of a child to self-determination of political beliefs and opinions is unconstitutional.

I will first state the main points of this argument and then develop the justification for them. First, a child has a constitutional right vis-à-vis his or her parents not to be subjected to an educational program that seeks to infringe the child's interest in political self-determination. Second, state law that authorizes parents to undertake this kind of instructional program is unconstitutional. Third, states have an affirmative obligation to protect children from the possibility that their parents may violate their right to political self-determination.

That children may have a constitutional right to be protected from parental action is not a new development in Constitutional law. The Supreme Court has already accepted the proposition that the mature female minor has a constitutional right to choose whether to have an abortion and that her parent, with the backing of state law, may not veto the exercise of this right (*Bellotti* v. *Baird,* 1979).

The case for the right itself rests on the insight that just as children are not "mere creatures of the State" (*Pierce* v. *Society of Sisters,* 1925, p. 534), neither are they the "mere creatures of their parents." For example, most people would agree that parental rights over children do not extend to denying children all formal education; children have a right to education (Olafson, 1973; Gutman, 1980). It is but a short step from this proposition to the additional conclusion that parents may not fulfill their obligations in such a way as to infringe upon children's right to political self-determination. The capacity for political self-determination is an important element of individual autonomy and is arguably necessary to achieve an extremely important good: self-realization or self-fulfillment (Feinberg, 1980, pp. 143–144). Furthermore, the capacity for self-determination of political beliefs and attitudes is an essential attribute of a citizen in a democracy, and parents who damage this capacity harm democratic government itself. Children who retain the capacity for political self-determination stand a better chance of not perpetuating such doctrines as Fascism and associated racist doctrines. That the child, if not properly inculcated, may turn against "acceptable" doctrine, as well, is undoubtedly a risk; but if the democratic principles of Jefferson are reasonable and persuasive, little is to be feared in accepting this risk.

The case for children's right to political self-determination rests on yet another line of argument. Parents must acknowledge their children's right to political self-determination if they claim the same right for themselves; consistency requires nothing less. But, it might be responded, children are different from adults. Hence, what the parents claim for themselves need not be claimed for their children. This argument, however, misses the point: What is being claimed for children is their right to self-determination when they become adults. Parents cannot deny to their children as adults what they claim for themselves as adults.

The child's right to political self-determination, furthermore, should take priority over whatever constitutionally based right parents may have to control the upbringing of children. It should be intuitively obvious that the right to self-determination is more basic and important to the individual and to society than is the liberty of a parent to achieve self-realization or self-fulfillment by denying that same possibility to a child.

The second proposition of this line of argument can now be established: Given the fundamental importance of the child's right to political self-determination, it follows that state law authorizing and supporting parental efforts to infringe on self-determination would be as unconstitutional as state law authorizing parents to veto abortion decisions of their minor daughters.

Although the second proposition is well supported, a more difficult point to support is the third, namely, that states have an affirmative obligation to protect children from the possibility that their parents may violate their right to political self-determination. This proposition is supported by the argument that closing off state courts to complaints by minors against their parents' educational programs would frustrate the realization of children's constitutional right and must itself be viewed as state support of unconstitutional behavior (Tribe, 1978, pp. 1152-1153).

The case for the Open Future Model is now complete. There are several important implications that follow from its acceptance as a correct interpretation of the Constitution. Judicial decisions such as *Ambach* v. *Norwick* (1979) and *Board of Education* v. *Pico* (1982), which rested on the proposition that public schools could engage in a program of inculcation, would have to be decided differently. And the decision in *Wisconsin* v. *Yoder* (1972) would undoubtedly have to be reversed. Positing a state duty to protect children from private efforts to inculcate would require states to expand their efforts to regulate private schools. More states might assert the authority to prohibit home instruction as a rational means to protect a child's right to an open political future. That is, states might be able to argue persuasively that ensuring that the child is educated among other children is a reasonable way of increasing the likelihood that the child will be exposed to political viewpoints beyond those of the parents (*State v. Eddington*, 1983).

Another significant implication of the Open Future Model would be for such cases as the one involving Walter Polovchak, the twelve-year-old Ukranian boy who, when his parents planned to return to the Soviet Union, ran away from his Chicago home to the home of a cousin and requested, with the aid of an attorney, political asylum in the United States (Fithian, 1984). Walter also filed a successful petition in state courts to have himself declared a ward of the state as a "minor in need of supervision." After the Polovchak parents returned to the Soviet Union without their son, and after years of litigation, the Illinois Supreme Court affirmed the Illinois Appellate Court decision that the trial judge's finding that Walter was in need of supervision was not supported by the evidence (*In re Polovchak*, 1984). Insofar as state law was concerned, the parents were entitled to custody of their son. Meanwhile, the Immigration and Naturalization Service had granted Walter asylum and issued on January 8, 1982, a departure-prevention order to prevent anyone's removing Walter from the country before the legal issues in the case could be resolved. The litigation over the question of asylum has continued, and two federal courts have concluded that the parents were denied procedural due process by the Immigration and Naturalization Service when it issued the departure-prevention order (*Polovchak* v. *Landon*, 1985). Now that Walter has turned eighteen, the many other legal issues in this case that remain unresolved may be moot, as he is no longer legally subject to the control of his parents and may himself legally apply for citizenship, a step he has said he will take. Most significant for these purposes, the central issue that will probably remain unresolved is the claim of the Polovchak parents that the granting of asylum to their son violated their parental rights.

Cases like the Polovchak case are too complex to discuss fully here; but, clearly, if the Constitution were understood to recognize a child's right of political self-determination, this would have an important bearing on resolving the question of whether a parent could forcibly repatriate a child to a country where the right to political self-determination is not recognized. If for no other reason, this right would have to be included in the calculus for determining whether the child's desire to remain in the United States would prevail over the parent's interest in retaining custody of the child in the country in which the parent prefers to live.

The Traditional and Open Future Models Reconsidered

My assessment of the Traditional and Open Future Models as interpretations of the Constitution begins by criticizing both for resting on methods of constitutional interpretation that are flawed in important respects.

The Traditional Model, as might be expected, assumes the Constitution was not intended to overturn basic traditional institutions and practices, such as the autonomy of the family and the authority of parents to control the upbringing of their children. The meaning of the Constitution is founded on the norms and principles of the existing institutions and practices of society. These institutions and practices are viewed with some reverence because they embody values and advantages that have stood the test of time; consequently, they should not be lightly tampered with, even in the name of more fully realizing the promise of abstract principles and reasons (compare Fishkin, 1983). Interpreters of this stripe believe the balance that the Constitution strikes between the liberty of the individual and the demands of society is the balance struck by the country, and an interpretation of the Constitution that departs from this tradition is not likely to survive long, while one that builds on it is likely to be sound (*Poe* v. *Ullman*, 1961, p. 542).

Advocates of the Open Future Model are likely to approach constitutional interpretation very differently. These interpreters pay allegiance to a set of basic, abstract, general principles. The principles are viewed as timeless—outside history, beyond culture, and rooted in a coherent social philosophy. This kind of interpreter tends to believe so fully in his social philosophy and the principles flowing from it that he urges that the Constitution itself be understood as embodying this philosophy and these principles (see, for example, Richards, 1980). Thus, as new legal conflicts arise, the legal rules adopted to settle disputes must implement the basic principles and values said to be in the Constitution. Existing institutions and practices are to be evaluated in light of these basic principles and values, and if they are found to be inconsistent, they must be deemed unconstitutional and must be changed, even if that means the repudiation of a tradition that has endured for centuries: "The established order has no claim to our allegiance just because it happens to exist, even if it has endured for a considerable period of time and affords a workably decent system of government. To have legitimacy, existing arrangements must conform to principles that can be 'deduced by pure reason' . . . ." (Kronman, 1985, p. 1601.)

Important difficulties are inherent in both these modes of interpretation. The first strongly tends to support the status quo and goes too far by rejecting the notion that the Constitution embodies fundamental principles, which may be used as a lever to change existing institutions, principles, and practices. Full adherence to this approach to constitutional interpretation would require reversing major constitutional decisions, which, although accepted now and relied upon by millions, could be viewed as illegitimate at the time of their adoption. In this connection, one need only consider the decision in *Brown* v. *Board of Education* (1954), which struck down the purposeful segregation of the races in the public schools. *Brown*, under this view, could be criticized for changing custom established in law and habit. The second approach tends to make judges into philosopher-kings, who are given a charter to make over the unruly world of politics and traditional institutions and practices so that they will conform to the judges' own philosophies of the right, the good, and the just. If permitted to act under such a conception of their role, judges would exacerbate beyond tolerance the difficulty that judicial review of the constitutionality of the acts of the other branches of government already entails: namely, that when the courts hold an executive or legislative act unconstitutional, they "thwart the will of the representatives of the actual people of the here and now" and "exercise control, not in behalf of the prevailing majority, but against it" (Bickel, 1962, p. 17).

Thus, the Traditional and Open Future interpretations of the Constitution rest on problematical approaches to constitutional interpretation. If a different—and, arguably, more acceptable—approach to constitutional interpretation were adopted, would we arrive at a different conception of the proper relationship among child-parent-state? I believe we would.

Let us look at an approach that might be viewed as a sort of hybrid—a cross between the two approaches just discussed. It begins, as does the first approach, with a search for traditional values and principles, but it approaches that search somewhat differently. This approach recognizes that our tradition includes many principles, values, and ideals that may not form a coherent whole. Political traditions may be "imprecise, inconsistent, and even partly unintelligible" (Kronman, 1985, p. 1603). Here, values and principles are ideals that may never be fully realized in practice. Furthermore, the interpretation of these principles would not be one that looked solely to tradition to ascertain their reach, scope, and weight. The judicial defense of rights would not be limited to prohibiting only those infringements that the framers of the Constitution would have condemned; it would extend to barring infringements in ways that accorded with contemporary understanding of the purpose of those rights ("Developments in the Law . . . ," 1980, p. 1180). The function, underlying purposes, and values of the principles would be chosen and used to apply the principles to new problems.

The courts may ("Developments in the Law . . . ," 1980, p. 1181) "adopt a functional approach to the right, letting its rationale dictate its scope." The principles would be given a consistent and principled interpretation, to be applied in a consistent and principled manner, and they could be used to reform even institutions that came to court with a long tradition; an effort might be made to close the gap between the ideal and reality. At the same time, existing institutions and practices would not automatically be viewed with suspicion but would be carefully examined to uncover the values they embodied and the extent of any real gap between the ideals and the institution. The importance these institutions and practices had in the lives of people and the good (and harm) they did would be understood before they were too quickly dismissed as being inconsistent with fundamental principles and rights. It would be remembered that ours is a tradition of many ideals, principles, and values, and that in many instances the tradition itself leaves open the question of the hierarchical ranking among principles, rights, and values.

If this approach were to be used in interpreting the Constitution, I believe that an interpretation different from both the Traditional and Open Future Models would emerge as the best interpretation of the Constitution. First, the new approach could be used to develop the line of argument used in connection with the Open Future Model, to restrict the public schools from indoctrinating pupils. This branch of the argument for the Open Future Model can be understood as resting on the intent of the framers, properly interpreted. If we interpret the intent of the framers of the free-speech clause of the First Amendment to be that of ensuring that our system is indeed a system of self-governance, then it follows that freedom of formation of belief is an essential right. Interpreting the First Amendment in this way employs the kind of functional approach discussed in the text: The scope of the right to free speech is being dictated by its rationale. Thus, at least this half of the Open Future Model would be accepted.

Second, our new approach would reject the line of argument developed on behalf of the second pillar of the Open Future Model, the restriction on parental authority to inculcate children. What emerges is the conclusion that although the public schools may not seek to infringe on the rights of children to political self-determination, parents may seek to do so. In brief, the Asymmetrical Model is the preferred interpretation of the Constitution.

This third approach to constitutional interpretation would examine, in a different way from the approach used in conjunction with the Open Future Model, the claim that children have a right not to be indoctrinated by their parents. First, it would stress that the Constitution has traditionally not been concerned with the relationship between private persons. Extending the Constitution in this way would open the door to a drastic expansion of the scope of legislative and judicial authority, which would violate many ideals, values, and principles of our political tradition. Second, an analyst using this approach would be careful to appreciate the values and advantages that lie behind the tradition of parents' authority over the upbringing of children. This analysis would undoubtedly reveal a line of thought supporting the view that parental directive education that sought to instill in children the parents' values worked, in the long term, to enhance the autonomy of the child and was a necessary basis for ultimate self-determination as an adult (Garvey, 1979). Given the dispute over this point, and our present uncertainty over the psychology of autonomy and self-determination (Sher and Bennett, 1982), an analyst working with this approach would treat with skepticism the claim that judicial and state intervention into the family is necessary to protect the child's right of political self-determination.

Putting aside the question of the appropriate method of constitutional interpretation and its use, there is yet another kind of criticism that can be leveled at the Open Future Model's call for judicial and legislative regulation of the family. Several prudential considerations counsel against acceptance of this dimension of the model. It would not be easy to limit state regulation of private education to the task of preserving the child's right to political self-determination. State regulation could easily overregulate and thereby infringe on basic constitutional rights and hinder the fostering of innovative and effective methods of education. Next, it is far from clear that state regulation would be effective in achieving its intended goal. The possibilities for evasion are too great, without a truly draconian regulatory effort. Finally, intrusive state regulation is bound to provoke bitter resentment and angry or even violent conflict between parents and the state. It is questionable that the resulting social schism would be worth the effort, especially given the fact that the claim on behalf of the child cannot be viewed as resting on an unconditional foundation.

In sum, I believe we are forced to the conclusion that only the Asymmetrical Model is an acceptable interpretation of the Constitution. The Traditional Model and the Open Future Model rest on methods of constitutional interpretation that are deeply flawed. The Traditional Model unnecessarily and without warrant infringes on the right of the student vis-à-vis government, and the Open Future Model represents too radical and dangerous a departure from tradition. Furthermore, the Asymmetrical Model, more strongly than the Traditional Model, embraces both the value of pluralism and diversity and a significant degree of wariness regarding governmental efforts to control the mind. But, although the Asymmetrical Model accepts as a matter of constitutional law the authority of parents to inculcate, it does not say such efforts are morally acceptable. On this question, the Asymmetrical Model adopts an "agnostic" position. This is a case in which what the Constitution permits is not necessarily moral. Thus, the Asymmetrical Model rests on at least one version of the doctrine of the separation of law and morals.

References

Ambach v. Norwick, 441 U.S. 68 (1979).
American Communications Association v. Douds, 339 U.S. 382 (1950).
Bellotti v. Baird, 443 U.S. 622 (1979).
Bickel, A. *The Least Dangerous Branch.* Indianapolis: Bobbs-Merrill, 1962.
Blum v. Yaretsky, 457 U.S. 991 (1982).
Board of Education Island Trees Union Free School District v. Pico, 457 U.S. 853 (1982).

Branti v. *Finkel,* 445 U.S. 507 (1980).
Brown v. *Board of Education,* 347 U.S. 483 (1954).
"Developments in the Law—The Constitution and the Family." *Harvard Law Review,* 1980, *93* (6), 1156-1383.
Elrod v. *Burns,* 427 U.S. 347 (1976).
Emerson, T. I. *The System of Freedom of Expression.* New York: Vintage, 1970.
Feinberg, J. "The Child's Right to an Open Future." In W. Aiken and H. LaFollette (eds.), *Whose Child?* Totowa, N.J.: Littlefield, Adams & Co., 1980.
Fishkin, J. S. *Justice, Equal Opportunity, and the Family.* New Haven, Conn.: Yale University Press, 1983.
Fithian, L. A. "Forcable Repatriation of Minors: The Competing Rights of Parent and Child." *Stanford Law Review,* 1984, *37,* 187-217.
Flagg Bros. Inc. v. *Brooks,* 436 U.S. 149 (1978).
Garvey, J. H. "Children and the First Amendment." *Texas Law Review,* 1979, *57* (3), 321-389.
Gutman, A. "Children, Paternalism, and Education." *Philosophy and Public Affairs,* 1980, *9* (4), 347-351.
In re Polovchak, 97 Ill.2d 212, 454 N.E.2d 258 (1983), *cert. denied,* 104 S.CT. 1413 (1984).
Jackson v. *Metropolitan Edison Co.,* 419 U.S. 345 (1974).
Keyishian v. *Board of Regents,* 385 U.S. 589 (1967).
Kronman, A. T. "Alexander Bickel's Philosophy of Prudence." *Yale Law Journal,* 1985, *94* (7), 1567-1616.
March v. *Alabama,* 326 U.S. 501 (1946).
Meyer v. *Nebraska,* 262 U.S. 390 (1923).
McLauglin, T. H. "Parental Rights and the Religious Upbringing of Children." *Journal of Philosophy of Education,* 1984, *18* (1), 75-83.
Nixon v. *Condon,* 286 U.S. 73 (1932).
Olafson, F. A. "Rights and Duties in Education." In J. F. Doyle (ed.), *Educational Judgments.* London: Routledge & Kegan Paul, 1973.
Orwell, G. *1984.* New York: Signet Classics, 1961.
Parham v. *J. R.,* 442 U.S. 584 (1979).
Pierce v. *Society of Sisters,* 268 U.S. 510 (1925).
Poe v. *Ullman,* 367 U.S. 497 (1961)(Harlan, J., dissenting).
Polovchak v. *Landon,* 614 F. Supp. 900 (N.D. Ill), *dismissed in part, vacated and remanded in part,* 774 F.2d 731 (7th Cir. 1985).
Plyler v. *Doe,* 457 U.S. 202 (1982).
Reynolds v. *United States,* 98 U.S. 145 (1878).
Richards, D. A. J. "The Individual, The Family, and the Constitution: A Jurisprudential Perspective." *New York University Law Review,* 1980, *55* (1), 1-62.
Runyon v. *McCrary,* 427 U.S. 160 (1976).
Scales v. *United States,* 367 U.S. 203 (1961).
Shelly v. *Kramer,* 334 U.S. 1 (1948).
Sher, G., and Bennett, W. J. "Moral Education and Indoctrination." *Journal of Philosophy,* 1982, *79* (11), 665-677.
Sherbert v. *Verner,* 374 U.S. 393 (1963).
State v. *Eddington,* 99 N.M. 715, 663 P.2d 374 (N.M. App. 1983), *cert. denied,* 104 S. Ct. 354 (1983).
Terry v. *Adams,* 345 U.S. 461 (1953).
Tribe, L. *American Constitutional Law.* Mineola, N.Y.: Foundation Press, 1978.
van Geel, T. "The Search for Constitutional Limits on Governmental Authority to Inculcate Youth." *Texas Law Review,* 1983, *62* (2), 197-297.

Wallace v. *Jaffree,* 86 L.Ed.2d 29 (1985).
West Virginia State Board of Education v. *Barnette,* 319 U.S. 624, 642 (1943).
Wisconsin v. *Yoder,* 406 U.S. 205 (1972).
Yates v. *United States,* 354 U.S. 298 (1957).

Tyll van Geel is a professor of education and political science at the University of Rochester. His research interests touch on a wide range of issues in educational law.

The Constitution provides the basis for principled resolutions to a number of current controversies involving children and education.

Children's Intellectual Rights: A First Amendment Analysis

David Moshman

"Congress shall make no law respecting an establishment of religion, or prohibiting the free exercise thereof; or abridging the freedom of speech, or of the press. . . ." In the United States, the Constitutional framework for intellectual rights lies in the opening words of the First Amendment. Not even a majority vote of duly elected representatives may violate basic freedoms of belief and expression. Moreover, the Fourteenth Amendment extends the scope of the First Amendment, such that state and local governments, as well as the federal government, are obliged to respect the intellectual rights guaranteed therein.

Nevertheless, there is considerable disagreement as to how far First Amendment rights extend. A strict constructionist interprets the First Amendment narrowly; a law or other government action would be struck down as unconstitutional only if it violated the First Amendment or some other portion of the Constitution in a clear and direct way. The problem

---

An earlier version of this chapter was presented at the meeting of the Jean Piaget Society, Philadelphia, June 1985. I am grateful to Bill Morris, Mario Scalora, Judy Newman, Bud Narveson, and Bridget Franks for comments on earlier drafts and helpful discussion of these issues. The views expressed, however, do not necessarily represent the views of any of the above individuals or of any organization with which I am associated.

with this is that application of a multifaceted document to complex and changing circumstances necessarily involves some degree of interpretation. If the interpretation is too narrow, there is danger of allowing all but the most blatant governmental infringements on precisely those intellectual rights the First Amendment was intended to protect.

A broader construction of the First Amendment construes it as setting greater limits on government. The problem in this case is that broad interpretations are necessarily somewhat subjective. Thus, there is danger of judges' thwarting the will of the majority on the basis of personal values and ideologies that they have read into the Constitution.

The present chapter takes a middle-ground approach. In deciding what actions are constitutionally protected, a considerable degree of interpretation is inevitable. The goal of such interpretation, however, should be to construe the Constitution in such a way that it is internally coherent and relevant to current circumstances. One must attempt to avoid interpretations that reconstruct the Constitution to fit a particular ideology or to reach a predetermined conclusion.

In the following pages, I proposed thirteen principles concerning children's intellectual rights. In accord with the approach just indicated, these principles are divided into two sets. The first set includes those that I believe follow from a reasonable interpretation of the First Amendment. I characterize these principles as addressing children's First Amendment rights.

Following the section on First Amendment rights, I present additional principles that I believe are consistent with the philosophy underlying the First Amendment, as well as with more general philosophical considerations. These principles go far enough beyond the language of the First Amendment, however, that they cannot, it seems to me, be considered inherent in it. Accordingly, we are not constitutionally required to act in accord with these further principles, although it would be wise, in my opinion, for us to do so.

Toward the end of the chapter, I will attempt to demonstrate the relevance of the principles proposed—and, more generally, the value of a principled approach—by using the principles to address a number of current controversies.

Rights Guaranteed by the First Amendment

The top half of Table 1 presents six principles of children's First Amendment rights. The first five are expressed in terms of limitations on government action. They reflect the common view that the First Amendment places restrictions on all levels of government, including public schools, but not on individuals acting in nongovernmental capacities (parents, private schools) (compare van Geel's Asymmetrical Model, this volume). The sixth principle places limits on the extent to which childhood status may be used to limit application of the first five principles.

Table 1. Children's First Amendment Rights

Rights Guaranteed by the First Amendment

1. *Free Expression.* Government may not hinder children from forming or expressing any idea unless the abridgment of belief or expression serves a compelling purpose that cannot be served in a less restrictive way.
2. *Freedom of Nonexpression.* Government may not require children to adopt or express a belief in any idea.
3. *Inculcation.* Government may inculcate ideas only when it has a legitimate purpose for doing so (for example, to produce educated citizens). Inculcation may not have the advancement or hindrance of any religion or of religion in general as its purpose or principal effect. Government may not indoctrinate children—that is, inculcate ideas in a way that unnecessarily limits the possibility of critical or rational analysis.
4. *Freedom of Access.* Government may not restrict a child's access to ideas and sources of information unless the restriction serves a compelling purpose that cannot be served in a less restrictive way.
5. *Free Exercise of Religion.* Government may not restrict children from acting in accord with their religious beliefs unless the restriction serves a compelling purpose (for example, to prevent disruption of education or perceived establishment of religion in a public school) that cannot be served in a less restrictive way.
6. *Distinction of Child from Adult.* Protection of children from harm due to their limited intellectual competence may be a compelling reason for limiting First Amendment rights, provided it can be shown that the children in question are less competent than the typical adult; the difference in competence is of such a nature and extent that substantial harm is likely unless First Amendment freedoms are abridged; and potential harm outweighs First Amendment interests.

Additional (Moral) Rights Consistent with First Amendment Philosophy

7. *Free Expression II.* Children have a right to form, express, and communicate any ideas.
8. *Freedom of Nonexpression II.* Children have a right not to adopt or express belief in ideas they do not wish to hold or express.
9. *Inculcation II.* Children have a right not to be subjected to inculcation, except for legitimate reasons, and not to be indoctrinated.
10. *Freedom of Access II.* Children have a right of access to all ideas and sources of information. Those responsible for their development have an affirmative obligation to provide access to diverse sources of information and to a reasonable diversity of opinions and perspectives.
11. *Free Exercise of Religion II.* Children have a right to act in accord with their religious beliefs except when restriction serves a compelling purpose (for example, to prevent harmful or illegal behavior) that cannot be served in a less restrictive way.
12. *Distinction of Child from Adult II.* Restrictions on children's intellectual rights should be limited to those necessitated by the individual child's circumstances and intellectual limitations.
13. *Right to Education.* To the extent that their rights are restricted on the basis of intellectual limitations, children have a right to the sort of environment that will facilitate their intellectual development and thus render such restriction unnecessary.

The first principle (*Free Expression*) follows directly from the First Amendment's assertion that government may not abridge freedom of speech or of the press. It includes the formation as well as the expression of ideas, since the right to express an idea is meaningless if one is prevented from forming or thinking about it. Note, however, that government does not have a First Amendment obligation to facilitate the formation or expression of ideas; it is merely forbidden to hinder the child. Note also that the principle allows for exceptions. If there is a compelling reason to limit expression of certain ideas (for example, disruption of classroom learning), limits may be imposed. There would, however, be a burden of proof on the government to show that it did have reason for the limitation, that the reason was sufficiently compelling to justify abridging a First Amendment right, and that there was no way to solve the problem that would have been less restrictive of children's rights.

The second principle (*Freedom of Nonexpression*) is closely related to the first. Freedom of expression implies not only freedom to form and express one's own ideas but also freedom not to adopt or express ideas of which one has not been convinced. Requiring a child to make a pledge or sing a song that expresses views contrary to his or her own would clearly be an abridgment of freedom of speech. This principle is stated in absolute terms. I cannot think of any case that would justify an exception.

Extending the first two principles, one is tempted to suggest that genuine respect for a child's freedom of belief and expression forbids the government to inculcate any ideas whatsoever. The ideal of government by the will of the people, after all, becomes meaningless if government is free to mold the will of the next generation via the public schools (van Geel, this volume). Government, one might argue, should be strictly content-neutral, leaving all judgments of truth or falsity up to children. Public education should present all ideas and facts and take no stand, thus avoiding inculcation.

Even cursory consideration of the nature of education immediately raises serious problems for this view. It is difficult to see how public education would be possible at all if government inculcation—that is, systematic efforts by public school teachers to get students to believe certain things without fully exploring reasons and options—were strictly forbidden. There simply is not time for full exploration of all topics, arguments, and alternatives. One might suggest that topic selection (for example, devoting more time to mathematics than to music) and inculcation of facts (for example, 2 + 2 = 4) should be permitted, but not inculcation of values. But this does not solve the problem. If a teacher believes that math is a valuable skill, and students perceive and adopt this view, then the teacher is inculcating a value.

Consideration of the nature of children increases the problem. Children, especially young children, show powerful inclinations to imitate what they observe and believe what they are told, particularly when the models or authorities are prestigious adults, such as teachers. It would be virtually impossible to be around a child for any length of time and not inculcate the child to some degree. Inculcation is simply unavoidable.

Accordingly, the third principle (*Inculcation*) does not forbid inculcation. Nevertheless, there is real reason to be concerned about government inculcation, especially—given compulsory education laws—in the public schools. The principle, therefore, includes three limitations.

First, government must have a legitimate basis for inculcation. It may be expected to show, for example, that there is educational value in the ideas it is inculcating. This is not as strict a standard as requiring a "compelling reason," but it does set some limit on governmental authority to inculcate whatever it pleases without justification.

Second, given the sensitivity of religious ideas and their explicit inclusion in the First Amendment, a much stronger limit on inculcation of religious ideas seems called for (compare Melton, this volume). The second sentence of Principle 3 severely restricts government inculcation of religion.

Finally, following Siegel (this volume), the principle recognizes a continuum extending from (relatively) noninculcative teaching through inculcation to indoctrination. In noninculcative teaching, a wide diversity of views and a range of information are presented; students are encouraged to pursue their interests and ideas and to express and justify their opinions. In inculcation, the teacher does not present students with the full range of reasons for believing something or with a full range of alternative ideas, because the time available is limited or because the students' cognitive abilities are too immature for them to grasp certain justifications or to grapple with competing points of view. In indoctrination, by contrast, reasons and alternatives are omitted because the government does not want the views it favors to be subjected to critical analysis or rational evaluation. In other words, although inculcation involves transmission of ideas and values without full appeal to the learner's critical rationality, indoctrination purposely and unnecessarily goes beyond this to short-circuit the possibility of rational analysis.

The last sentence of the principle absolutely forbids indoctrination. It recognizes that it is often necessary to inculcate ideas in a way that limits or at least fails to encourage questioning. Public school teachers must decide what topics, views, arguments, and information to teach, and what to omit, on the basis of professional judgments about what is important for children to learn and about what they are intellectually capable of understanding. In presenting ideas, however, they may neither withhold contradictory evidence, alternative ideas, or relevant contrary arguments nor discourage questions or critical observations simply because the government wishes to direct students' minds toward certain beliefs. Government restrictions on critical analysis go beyond inculcation to indoctrination when they cannot be justified on educational grounds. Teachers must recognize limitations in students' critical thinking abilities but must not systematically educate them in such a way as to hinder the development of their rational competencies and, thus, their abilities to exercise freedoms of belief and expression.

The fourth principle (*Freedom of Access*) raises equally complex issues. It relates to what is often termed a *right to know*.

It is clear that access to a variety of information sources and to a diversity of opinions and perspectives plays an important role in formulating one's own ideas and that formulation of ideas is necessary to expressing them. Moreover, freedom of expression obviously becomes meaningless if government can prevent access to one's ideas. Thus, although the First Amendment refers to expression rather than to receipt of ideas, it strongly entails a right to receive as well.

It would go too far, however, to say that people have a positive First Amendment right to express or to know. In forbidding abridgment of free expression, the First Amendment does not require government to facilitate expression (for example, by providing financial support for publication). Similarly, with respect to receipt of ideas, government is not affirmatively obligated to provide a child with every idea anyone has expressed. It simply may not take action to restrict his or her access.

Although the right to know is thus limited, the Freedom of Access principle nevertheless accords it a meaningful status. Government may (actively) restrict a child's access to ideas or materials only when it can demonstrate a compelling reason for doing so.

The fifth principle (*Free Exercise of Religion*) follows the First Amendment in noting that a child not only has the right to hold and express certain religious beliefs but also has the right to act on them—that is, to behave as his or her religion requires. Since behavior, more than speech, has the potential to interfere with the rights of others, however, the right to free exercise cannot be absolute. One might need to limit it in a public school, for example, if a child were doing things that interfered with the education of others in the class or if children engaged in activities that created the impression that the school had endorsed a particular religion (thus presenting an establishment-of-religion problem with respect to other children). To limit a child's free exercise of religion, however, the government must show that there is compelling reason to do so and that the limitation is the least restrictive of those available.

The first five principles are stated in terms of limitations on governmental action. It is specified, however, that most of these limitations are not absolute. Government may inculcate ideas to a considerable extent, and it may limit children's freedom of expression, access to ideas, and free exercise of religion to the extent that it can demonstrate a compelling interest in doing so. The compelling-interest standard is stiff but not insurmountable. In specifying that such a standard must be met to deny children First Amendment protections, it is implied that childhood status is not in itself a compelling reason for denial of rights.

The issue of childhood status as a basis for denying rights is sufficiently important to merit a principle of its own. The sixth principle (*Distinction of Child from Adult*) recognizes that the usual justification for limiting children's freedoms more than those of adults is that children have limited intellectual competence and are therefore more likely not to act in their own best interests. They are thus likely to suffer harm unless their freedoms are limited. The principle accepts this rationale but puts the burden of proof on the government to show that the asserted difference in competence does exist and does result in sufficiently serious risk to justify abridging fundamental rights.

This analysis views children as—in a legal sense—persons. It assumes that the First Amendment applies to all people and then proceeds, with caution, to the recognition of exceptions. This approach can be justified on the (strict constructionist) grounds that the Bill of Rights nowhere distinguishes children from adults; it refers only to "people" and "persons." The literal language of the First Amendment constrains all government interference with freedom of religion and expression.

It might be argued that, although the literal language of the First Amendment encompasses all people, the writers did not have children in mind. It is equally true, however, that they were not considering women or blacks either. Given the Fourteenth Amendment's guarantee of equal protection under the law, to construe the First Amendment today as limited to white male adults would render the Constitution incoherent.

It might also be argued that the First Amendment, although referring generally to "freedom of speech or of the press," was really intended to guarantee open political discourse, rather than expression in a more general sense. Accordingly, one might argue, it is relevant only with respect to voting adults. It follows, then, that the First Amendment, if it applies to children at all, is less important to them than to adults; the standard for making exceptions should thus be correspondingly less stringent.

A major problem with this argument is its facile assumption that political and nonpolitical issues are easily distinguished. On the contrary, many political controversies hinge largely on where one draws the line between the personal and the political. To limit the First Amendment to political matters and then give government the authority to determine what issues are legitimately political would strangle the First Amendment.

Moreover, even if one is concerned only with adult liberties, it is critical to keep in mind that children turn into adults and that what they can think and express as adults depends in part on their experiences as children. There is substantial evidence that exposure to diverse points of view and encouragement to form, express, and discuss one's own opinions are crucial to intellectual development (Bearison, Magzamen, and Filardo, 1986; Berkowitz, 1985; Johnson and Johnson, 1985; Walker, 1983). When one denies an adult access to diverse ideas, one is restricting available input; when one denies such access to a child, however, one is also restricting development of the ability to coordinate differing views. When one denies an adult free expression, one is denying the opportunity to communicate; when one denies free expression to a child, however, one is also restricting development of the ability to form one's own ideas. In short, in denying First Amendment rights to a child, one is restricting not merely the present exercise of those rights but also the further development of precisely those intellectual competencies that make the First Amendment meaningful. Contrary to the suggestion that children have little at stake, it appears that as future adults they may have more to lose than present adults from governmental restriction of their intellectual freedoms.

It should be noted in passing that less than full respect for the First Amendment rights of students in public schools creates a special problem of its own. One of the major rationales for compulsory education is the need to develop good citizens. Presumably, good citizenship in the United States includes understanding of and respect for the Bill of Rights. Students can hardly be expected to learn this, however, if school officials demonstrate by their actions that they believe the First Amendment is primarily a threat to public order and should be applied as restrictively as they can get away with. On the contrary, public schools should take particular care to demonstrate governmental respect for freedom of religion and expression (Franks, this volume).

Although the case for construing children as people with respect to First Amendment rights seems strong, Principle 6 nevertheless acknowledges that the limited intellectual competence of children may justify distinguishing them from adults. It mandates, however, that any proposed limitation of rights be supported by a demonstration of likely harm due to limited intellectual competence. Obviously, it would be unreasonable to demand the sort of clear proof that research in the social sciences simply cannot provide. Nevertheless, psychological research on children and development is sufficiently advanced to provide some real guidance (Melton, this volume). We should certainly require a case based on empirical evidence, rather than relying on intuition and speculation. (For a systematic review of psychological research on the development of reasoning, with emphasis on legal applications, see Moshman, forthcoming.)

It might be argued that, in cases of doubt, government should err on the side of protecting children from harming themselves (compare Wringe, this volume). There are problems with this, however. First, it must be kept in mind that government protection is not the only or even the major protection children have. On the contrary, our society relies primarily on parents to protect children from reading harmful materials or forming dangerous beliefs. For government to step in and play a role in this task raises serious threats, not only to children's rights but also to the rights of parents. Government should indeed have the power to do this, but it is reasonable to expect it to meet a high standard of evidence in proving its compelling interest in any particular case.

It is also important to note that although allowing children too much freedom may put them at risk, there is also risk in restricting them too much. The First Amendment embodies the philosophy that government restriction poses dangers of its own that may be greater than the dangers it is intended to avoid. It is not obvious that in any case of doubt we should err on the side of protecting children from dangerous options and harmful ideas; we may in fact be shielding them from perspectives and possibilities that would be intellectually liberating in the long run. When evidence is lacking or ambiguous, the Bill of Rights requires government to err on the side of too much freedom rather than on the side of unnecessary restriction.

One more point should be made about the interpretation of evidence concerning children's competencies. Since constitutional rights apply to all normal adults, the competence of normal adults, rather than some rational ideal, is taken in Principle 6 as the constitutionally relevant standard.

Additional Rights

The bottom portion of Table 1 presents seven additional principles. Although these are consistent with the general philosophy of intellectual freedom underlying the First Amendment, they go too far beyond the actual language of the First Amendment to be considered constitutional guarantees. They do, however, correspond to the sorts of intellectual rights that both Siegel and Wringe (this volume) justify on moral grounds. They may thus be considered moral rather than legal rights.

Principles 7 through 11 correspond, respectively, to the intellectual rights of Principles 1 through 5. They differ in three major respects. First, they take the form "Children have a right . . ." rather than "Government may not. . . ." Clearly, the framers of the Bill of Rights placed limits on governmental action, not to punish it for historical infractions, but rather to protect the rights of people not to be limited in certain ways. Whether a child is indoctrinated by the government or by his or her parents is irrelevant from the point of view of the child's access to the intellectual world. Thus, we should construe the underlying philosophy of the First Amendment as providing for certain intellectual rights. Only the government is constitutionally required to respect these rights (compare van Geel's Asymmetrical Model), but private individuals, including parents, have corresponding moral obligations.

A second difference between the rights in the two sets is that the second set is expressed more absolutely, with fewer qualifications. There are, of course, limitations on rights in the latter set corresponding to those noted in the former set, and it would have been possible to write these into the principles. Not doing so, however, has the advantage of reminding us that even when denial of a certain right is justifiable, it is nevertheless regrettable—a freedom has been abridged. It may be appropriate not to allow a nine-year-old to read certain things, but it is unfortunate when this is necessary. It follows that in limiting children's intellectual rights on the grounds of lack of competence, we incur a moral obligation to facilitate the development of those competencies that would make such denial of rights unnecessary (Principle 13, *Right to Education*).

There is a third distinction between the rights in the two sets: Whereas those in the first set are entirely negative rights—that is, rights not to have certain things done to you—the second set includes an affirmative obligation to expose children to diverse perspectives and sources of information (Principle 10). This reflects a broader "right to know." Parents have moral obligations to children's intellectual development that go beyond anything that either they or the government are constitutionally required to do.

Principle 12 (*Distinction of Child from Adult II*) differs from its counterpart in the first set (Principle 6) primarily in its greater emphasis on individualized determination. To the extent that the government limits rights on the basis of intellectual competence, it would typically do this for groups of children (for example, removing a book from an elementary school library on the basis of evidence that it is harmful to children under age twelve). Parents, however, should be more sensitive to the individual characteristics of their own children, who may be more or less advanced than their peers in their ability to deal with conflicting opinions or make sense of certain types of issues.

To the extent that the second set of rights goes beyond the first, the government is not constitutionally required to respect them. Nevertheless, it may do so if it chooses, and a strong case can be made that it is wise social policy for government to go farther than required in actively protecting and encouraging freedoms of religion and expression. In fact, government may sometimes be justified in asserting that it has a compelling interest in furthering children's intellectual opportunities and should thus be permitted to do so, even at the expense of parental rights to direct the development of their own children. Compulsory education, for example, seems to me to require a rationale of this sort.

In sum, there is a broad range of possibilities in between what government is constitutionally required to do and what it is constitutionally forbidden to do. Government may—and, in my opinion, should—use First Amendment values of intellectual freedom as a basis for choosing educational policies within the optional area. Moreover, if those policies are challenged as conflicting with other fundamental (parental) rights, government may in some cases justify them by demonstrating a compelling interest in furthering the intellectual development of young citizens.

Applications

In this section, I address some current issues in education. Although each deserves much more thorough analysis, the presentation will suffice to show the range of issues to which the present principles are relevant.

Censorship of Student Speech and Publications. Principle 1 suggests that exceptional justification (for example, clear and direct disruption of the education of other students) should be required for censorship of student expression by public school officials.

Student-Initiated Groups. The Equal Access Act of 1984 requires that if a public secondary school makes its facilities available to students for extracurricular activities, it must allow equal access to all student groups, regardless of the religious, political, or philosophical content of their activities. Opponents of school prayer have feared that this bill will open public schools to religious activities. Others have feared that the bill will open schools to young Nazis, communists, homosexuals, and other groups.

The Equal Access Act protects the right of students to express and be exposed to views the government dislikes (Principles 1 and 4). It is, of course, important to be sure that adults are not using school facilities to indoctrinate student groups (Principle 3), that students are not being coerced into joining such groups (Principle 2), and that students are not incorrectly perceiving that the views of groups using school facilities are officially approved by school authorities (Principle 3). Although these are real dangers that must be monitored, they should not blind us to the genuine potential of the Equal Access Act for increasing the intellectual opportunities of secondary students (Principles 7, 10, 11).

Censorship of Textbooks and School Libraries. Public schools have been the targets of continuing efforts to censor what children read and hear (Jenkinson, 1986; Moshman, 1981). Although such efforts are primarily associated with the religious right (Moral Majority, Eagle Forum, and similar groups), they are not limited to any religion or ideology. It is important to note that schools must make choices; they cannot use every text or stock every book in the library. Selections should, however, be made in accord with educationally relevant, written criteria aimed at providing as wide a variety of views and ideas as students can handle (Principle 3). Removals should follow carefully designed procedures in which these criteria are carefully applied (Principle 4) and claims of harm based on alleged lack of cognitive competence are seriously scrutinized (Principle 6).

Value Neutrality. It is often suggested that public schools should be value-neutral. Strict value-neutrality is impossible and probably undesirable. If cheating is forbidden, for example, the school is supporting intellectual honesty; if students' First Amendment rights are protected, the school is promoting constitutional values. Nevertheless, departures from value-neutrality should be open to scrutiny to ensure that they have educational rather than religious or other partisan purposes and avoid indoctrination by presenting as much diversity and encouraging as much questioning as is feasible, given other curricular demands and the cognitive levels of the students (Principle 3).

Government Regulation of Private and Home Schools. Many states regulate private schools—for example, by mandating teacher certification or curriculum standards. Such regulation is not constitutionally required but is permissible if it is necessary to protect children's right to a nonindoctrinative education (Principle 9), one that facilitates their intellectual development (Principles 7 and 10). Regulation for the purpose of indoctrinating children in a particular ideology, however, violates the rights of children (Principle 3) and parents alike (Arons, 1983). Thus, a given regulation is legitimate if and only if it serves a compelling educational purpose and that purpose cannot be served with a less restrictive regulation (Moshman, 1985a).

"Scientific" Creationism. Proponents of creationism—the view that all species were created 10,000 years ago, as described in *Genesis*—have proposed that their view is a scientific theory and should be given equal weight whenever the theory of evolution is taught. Respect for children's rights does not require that we give equal weight to every point of view or that we ignore legitimate standards of scientific adequacy in making curriculum decisions (Principle 3). To the extent allowed by children's cognitive competence, however (Principle 6), education in evolution should avoid indoctrination by stressing empirical evidence and scientific reasoning (Principle 3), rather than relying on appeals to authority (Principle 3) and censorship of creationist views (Principle 4) (Moshman, 1985b). It should be clear to students that although they will be expected to understand the theory of evolution, they are not required to believe it (Principle 2).

The Antihumanist Movement. Many fundamentalist Christians argue that secular humanism is a religion and is being taught in the public schools (Moshman, 1981). Secular humanists, they claim, espouse an atheistic philosophy, in which children are taught to rely on their own reasoning rather than on the word of God. Systematically inculcating an atheistic philosophy would violate the establishment-of-religion clause of the First Amendment (Principle 3). Simply teaching students to reason, however, serves a legitimate educational purpose and does not violate the First Amendment, even if it involves inculcation of the idea that reasoning about problems is a good way to solve them (Principle 3).

Prayer in Public Schools. Students have a First Amendment right to pray in accord with their religious beliefs, provided they do not disrupt the education of other students (Principle 5). For the school to organize time for prayer, however, or to set up "moments of silence" in order to encourage prayer, is an unacceptable inculcation of religion (Principle 3) (Melton, this volume). Even when prayer groups are genuinely student-organized, there is the danger that other students will perceive an establishment of religion (Principle 3). With older children, it may be possible explicitly to note the nonendorsement of the school in order to minimize the establishment problem and thus permit free exercise by the religious students (Principle 5). The distinction between student activities on school premises and official school activities may be too subtle, however, for younger children to grasp (Principle 6), in which case some restriction on free exercise may be constitutionally acceptable or even required (Principle 5).

Conclusion

Although it has been firmly established since 1969 that children have First Amendment rights (*Tinker* v. *Des Moines Independent Community School District*, 1969), there is much confusion in the courts as to what this entails and how far it extends. Some decisions have been in accord with the principles proposed in this chapter, but others have not. The present work should thus be seen as a proposal concerning what rights of children the courts and the public schools ought to recognize under the First Amendment, not as a summary of what rights they currently do recognize. Detailed analysis of actual cases and decisions with reference to the current principles would be beyond the scope of this chapter (but see Moshman, forthcoming).

It is possible to disagree with this chapter on several levels. One might, for example, reach different conclusions in applying the principles to some of the issues discussed. The political and financial realities of public schools often make application of ideal principles difficult and make compromise unavoidable (Franks, this volume). Moreover, many educational controversies require careful balancing of two or more interests, rights, or principles, and there may be legitimate disagreement as to the most appropriate solutions (Moshman, 1985a).

On a more basic level, one might disagree with the principles themselves or with the categories to which I have assigned them. A strict constructionist critique of the present chapter would attempt to demonstrate that some or all of the principles that I propose as constitutional do not follow directly from the First Amendment. Thus, the rights they involve, even if morally genuine, are not constitutional rights. A broad constructionist critique, in contrast, would try to show that I have been too narrow in interpreting the First Amendment, and that some or all of the rights I see as merely consistent with an underlying First Amendment philosophy are in fact directly implicated in the First Amendment and thus constitutionally protected (compare the Open Future Model described by van Geel, this volume).

It is possible, however, to disagree with some or all of the specific principles and still accept the underlying approach this chapter illustrates. My general proposition is that a variety of current controversies involving children and education, although quite different from one another, are best addressed not on an ad hoc basis but rather through systematic application of principles derived from the First Amendment. I have changed my opinion about some of the specific principles and may do so again; my deeper message is the power of a principled approach.

References

Arons, S. *Compelling Belief: The Culture of American Schooling.* New York: McGraw-Hill, 1983.

Bearison, D. J., Magzamen, S., and Filardo, E. K. "Socio-cognitive Conflict and Cognitive Growth in Young Children." *Merrill-Palmer Quarterly,* 1986, *32,* 51-72.

Berkowitz, M. W. (ed.). *Peer Conflict and Psychological Growth.* New Directions for Child Development, no. 29. San Francisco: Jossey-Bass, 1985.

Jenkinson, E. *The Schoolbook Protest Movement: Forty Questions and Answers.* Bloomington, Ind.: Phi Delta Kappa Educational Foundation, 1986.

Johnson, D. W., and Johnson, R. "Classroom Conflict: Controversy Versus Debate in Learning Groups." *American Educational Research Journal,* 1985, *22,* 237-256.

Moshman, D. "Jean Piaget Meets Jerry Falwell: Genetic Epistemology and the Anti-humanist Movement in Education." *The Genetic Epistemologist,* 1981, *10* (3), 10-13.

Moshman, D. "*Faith Christian* v. *Nebraska:* Parent, Child, and Community Rights in the Educational Arena." *Teachers College Record,* 1985a, *86,* 553-571.

Moshman, D. "A Role for Creationism in Science Education." *Journal of College Science Teaching,* 1985b, *15,* 106-109.

Moshman, D. *Children's First Amendment Rights.* Lincoln: University of Nebraska Press, forthcoming.

Tinker v. *Des Moines Independent Community School District,* 393 U.S. 503 (1969).

Walker, L. J. "Sources of Cognitive Conflict for Stage Transition in Moral Development." *Developmental Psychology,* 1983, *19,* 103-110.

David Moshman is associate professor of educational psychology at the University of Nebraska-Lincoln, and first vice-president of the Nebraska Civil Liberties Union. His primary research interests are intellectual rights of children and students and development of reasoning during adolescence and beyond.

Do children have the right to education for critical thinking? Do we as educators have a corresponding obligation to help students become capable, independent, autonomous thinkers? Why?

Critical Thinking as an Intellectual Right

Harvey Siegel

Philosophers and educational theorists have long held that a central aim of education is the fostering of rationality, or critical thought. According to this view, a well-educated person is one who is able to think well—to evaluate claims and arguments put forward by others, to reasonably formulate his or her own beliefs, and to act and be disposed to act in accordance with the dictates of reason. At present, there is a significant amount of work, both theoretical and practical, being done on behalf of critical thinking. Curricula are being formulated, programs developed, and tests constructed, all aimed at the educational enhancement of critical thinking. At the same time, theorists are attempting to refine the concept of critical thinking, to define its proper role in education, and to justify it as an educational ideal.

This chapter is adapted from Siegel (in press), in which I argue that the critical thinker is best thought of as one who is appropriately moved by reasons. In this view, critical thinking involves a variety of reasoning and other cognitive skills; knowledge of various sorts; a set of tendencies or dispositions to exercise those skills and utilize that knowledge; the valuing of reasons and an appreciation of their epistemological force; and a certain sort of character. I am grateful to David Moshman and Carol Crowley for helpful comments on an earlier draft.

One way to justify critical thinking as an educational ideal is to conceive of it as an intellectual right. In this conception, critical thinking is a legitimate and, indeed, central educational ideal, because children have the right—the intellectual right—to an education aimed at the fostering or enhancing of critical thinking. That is, children have the right to the opportunity to become, insofar as they are able, critical thinkers.

Note that the right in question involves the opportunity to become a critical thinker, rather than a right to *be* a critical thinker. We cannot say that children have the right to be or become critical thinkers, any more than persons can have the right to be champion swimmers, gifted painters, or brilliant mathematicians. Native ability and personal effort play important roles in a person's actually becoming any of these things. What children may be said to have a right to is an opportunity to become critical thinkers, insofar as they are able. They have, therefore, not the right to be or become critical thinkers, but rather the right to an education that aims at fostering critical thinking. In what follows, "the right to be or become a critical thinker" should be taken as shorthand for "the right to an education that aims at fostering or enhancing critical thinking."

Can education for critical thinking appropriately be conceived of as an intellectual right? In what follows, I will argue that it can. I will argue, that is, that there are good reasons for believing that children have the right to an education that fosters critical thinking, and that educators have a corresponding obligation to help students become critical thinkers.

The Right to Be a Critical Thinker

Why should we think that the child has a right to an education aimed at the development of a certain sort of intellect, the right to an education for critical thinking? In what follows, I offer four reasons for thinking so.

Respect for Students as Persons. The first reason involves our moral obligations to students and is most directly relevant to the portion of critical thinking that has to do with the manner of teaching. That is, it purports to justify the claim that students have the right to be taught in the critical manner, which amounts to the right to be taught so as to become critical thinkers.

The *critical manner* is the manner of teaching that fosters critical thinking. A teacher who utilizes the critical manner seeks to encourage in his or her students the skills, habits, and dispositions necessary for the development of what may be called the critical spirit (compare Siegel, in press). This means, first, that the teacher always recognizes the right of the student to question and demand reasons and consequently recognizes an obligation to provide reasons whenever they are demanded. The critical manner thus demands of a teacher a willingness to subject all beliefs and practices to scrutiny, so as to allow students the genuine opportunity to understand the role reasons play in the justification of thought and action. The critical manner also demands honesty of a teacher: Reasons presented by a teacher must be genuine reasons, and the teacher must honestly appraise the power of those reasons. In addition, the teacher must submit her reasons to the independent evaluation of the student:

> To teach ... is at some points at least to submit oneself to the understanding and independent judgment of the pupil, to his demand for reasons, to his sense of what constitutes an adequate explanation. To teach someone that such and such is the case is not merely to try to get him to believe it: deception, for example, is not a method or a mode of teaching. Teaching involves further that, if we try to get the student to believe that such and such is the case, we try also to get him to believe it for reasons that, within the limits of his capacity to grasp, are *our* reasons. Teaching, in this way, requires us to reveal our reasons to the student and, by so doing, to submit them to his evaluation and criticism [Scheffler, 1960, p. 57].

Teaching in the critical manner is thus teaching so as to develop in students the skills and attitudes consonant with critical thinking. It is, as Scheffler puts it, an attempt to initiate students "into the rational life, a life in which the critical quest for reasons is a dominant and integrating motive" (Scheffler, 1965, p. 107).

Since being taught in the critical manner amounts to being taught so as to become a critical thinker, an obligation to teach in the critical manner constitutes a recognition of an obligation to teach so as to foster critical thinking. This latter obligation in turn involves a recognition of students' intellectual right to be so taught. And we are in fact obliged to teach in the critical manner. We are so obliged simply because we are morally obliged to treat students (and everyone else) with respect. If we are to conduct our interpersonal affairs morally, we must recognize and honor the fact that we are dealing with other persons, who as such deserve respect—that is, we must show respect for persons. This includes the recognition that other persons are of equal moral worth, which entails that we treat other persons in such a way that their moral worth is respected. This in turn requires that we recognize the needs, desires, and legitimate interests of other persons to be as worthy of consideration as our own. In our dealings with other persons, we must not grant our interests any more weight, simply because they are *our* interests, than we grant the interests of others. The concept of respect for persons is a Kantian one, for it was Kant who urged that we treat others as ends and not as means (Kant, 1959). This involves recognizing the equal worth of all persons. Such worth is the basis of the respect that all persons are owed (compare Scheffler, 1985).

It is important to note that respect for persons has ramifications far beyond the realm of education. All persons in all situations deserve to be treated with respect, to be regarded as morally significant and worthy entities. This general point includes educational situations, since educational situations involve persons. Here is the relevance to education of the Kantian conception of respect for persons. It is also worth pointing out that the obligation to treat students with respect is independent of more specific educational aims. It is an obligation binding on us generally and so is not part of any particular educational setting or system. Whatever else we are trying to do in our educational institutions, we are obliged to treat students with respect.

What does it mean for a teacher to recognize the equal moral worth of students and to treat them with respect? Among other things, it means recognizing and honoring students' right to question, challenge, and demand reasons and justifications for what is being taught. The teacher who fails to recognize these rights of students fails to treat them with respect, for treating students with respect involves recognizing students' right to exercise independent judgment and powers of evaluation. To deny students this right is to deny them the status of "persons of equal moral worth." To treat students with respect is, moreover, to be honest with them. To deceive, indoctrinate, or otherwise fool students into believing anything, even if it is true, is to fail to treat them with respect. The Kantian principle of respect for persons thus requires that we treat students in a certain manner, one that honors students' demands for reasons and explanations, deals with students honestly, and recognizes the need to confront students' independent judgment.

Thus, the general moral requirement to treat persons with respect applies to the teacher's dealings with her students, simply because those students are persons and so are deserving of respect. It is independent of any specific educational aim. Nevertheless, it offers justification for conceiving of a critical thinking-oriented education as a student's intellectual right in that the way one teaches, according to the critical manner, is in crucial respects isomorphic to the way one teaches so as to respect students. In both, the student's right to question, challenge, and seek reasons, explanations, and justifications must be respected. In both, the teacher must deal honestly with the student. In both, the teacher must submit reasons for taking some claim to be true or some action to be justified to the student's independent judgment and critical scrutiny. In most respects, then, teaching in the critical manner is simply teaching in such a way as to treat students with respect. The obligation to treat students with the respect they are due as persons thus constitutes a reason for adopting the critical manner. In short, this manner of teaching is morally required. It is also part and parcel of the ideal of critical thinking. Thus, morality provides one powerful reason for operating our educational institutions, and conducting our educational affairs more generally, in ways that accord with that ideal. Concomitantly, morality provides a reason for regarding treatment that fosters critical thinking as a child's intellectual right.

Self-Sufficiency and Preparation for Adulthood. The second reason for taking critical thinking to be an intellectual right has to do with education's generally recognized task of preparing students to become competent with respect to those abilities necessary for the successful management of adult life. We educate, at least in part, in order to prepare children for adulthood, but we cannot say in advance that Johnny will be a pilot, for example, and arrange his education accordingly, for Johnny may well decide to be something else. In general, when we say that education prepares children for adulthood, we do not mean for some specific adult role. Rather, we mean that education strives to enable children to face adulthood successfully.

In particular, we hope that education fosters in children the power and ability to control, insofar as they are able, their own lives. We guide a child's education primarily because the child cannot responsibly guide it herself, but we seek to bring her, as quickly as possible, to the point at which she can "take over the reins" and guide her own education and life generally. That is, we seek to render the child self-sufficient; to empower the student to control her destiny and create her future (compare Scheffler, 1973). To get the student to the point at which she can competently control her own life and responsibly contribute to social life is to bring the student into the adult community, to recognize the student as a fellow member of a community of equals. To thus empower the student is to raise her, in the most appropriate sense of the term, to her fullest potential, for any such potential surely includes the power to shape and choose, and to attain, possible potentials (compare Scheffler, 1985). Indeed, this is a fundamental obligation to children. Without proper education, children would not get to the point at which they could competently control their own destinies; many options would be forever closed to them because of their poor training. To meet our obligation to prepare children well for adulthood, we must strive to educate them in such a way that they are maximally self-sufficient.

How can we organize educational activities so as to empower the student? My suggestion, predictably enough, is that we organize those activities according to the dictates of critical thinking. To help students to become critical thinkers is to "encourage them to ask questions, to look for evidence, to seek and scrutinize alternatives, to be critical of their own ideas as well as those of others" (Scheffler, 1973, p. 143). Such encouragement conforms well to the effort to encourage self-sufficiency, since, as Scheffler puts it, "This educational course precludes taking schooling as an instrument for shaping [students'] minds to a preconceived idea. For if they seek reasons, it is their evaluation of such reasons that will determine what ideas they eventually accept" (Scheffler, 1973, p. 143). By encouraging critical thinking, then, we teach the student what we think is right, but we encourage the student to scrutinize our reasons and judge independently the rightness of our claims. In this way the student becomes a competent judge; more important for the present point, the student becomes an independent judge. That is, the student makes her own judgments regarding the appropriateness of alternative beliefs, courses of action, and attitudes. Such competence and independence of judgment are the sine qua non of self-sufficiency. The self-sufficient person is, moreover, a liberated person; such a person is free from the unwarranted and undesirable control of unjustified beliefs, unsupportable attitudes, and paucity of abilities, which can prevent that person from competently taking charge of her own life. Critical thinking thus liberates as it renders students self-sufficient (compare Scheffler, 1973). Insofar as we recognize our obligation to help children become competent, self-sufficient adults, that obligation provides a justification for the ideal of critical thinking, since education conceived along the lines suggested by that ideal recognizes obligation explicitly. Here, then, is a second reason for taking critical thinking to be a legitimate educational ideal and education for critical thinking to be a fundamental intellectual right of children.

Initiation into the Rational Traditions. As argued elsewhere (Siegel, in press), critical thinking is best seen as coextensive with rationality, and rationality is concerned with reasons. For a person to be rational, that person must (at least) grasp the relevance of various reasons for judgments and evaluate the weight of such reasons properly. How does a person learn to evaluate reasons properly?

One plausible account suggests that a person learns the proper assessment of reasons by being initiated into the traditions in which reasons play a role. Education, in this view, centrally involves the initiation of the student into the central human traditions (Peters, 1972). These traditions—science, literature, history, the arts, mathematics, and so on—have developed, over their long history, guidelines concerning the role and nature of reasons in their respective domains. Thus, for example, a science student must learn, among other things, what counts as a good reason for or against some hypothesis, theory, or procedure; how much weight the reason has; and how it compares with other relevant reasons. Science education amounts, at least ideally, to initiating the student into the scientific tradition, which in part consists in appreciating that tradition's standards governing the appraisal of reasons (McPeck, 1981, pp. 155-158). Similar remarks apply to other curricular areas.

If we can take education to involve significantly the initiation of students into the rational traditions, and if such initiation consists in part in helping the student to appreciate the standards of rationality that govern the assessment of reasons (and so proper judgment) in each tradition, then we have a third reason for regarding critical thinking as an educational ideal and education for critical thinking as an intellectual right. Critical thinking, we have seen, involves a recognition of the importance of getting students to understand and appreciate the role of reasons in rational endeavor and of fostering in students those traits, attitudes, and dispositions that encourage the seeking of reasons for grounding judgment, belief, and action. Understanding the role and criteria of evaluation of reasons in the several rational traditions is crucial to being successfully initiated into those traditions. If education involves initiation into the rational traditions, then we should take critical thinking to be an educational ideal and education for critical thinking to be an intellectual right, because so taking it involves fostering in students those traits, dispositions, attitudes, and skills that are conducive to the successful initiation of students into the rational traditions. Seeing education as initiation thus offers justification for the ideal of critical thinking and for the recognition of education for critical thinking as an intellectual right of children. So long as children are entitled to be educated, they are entitled to education that seeks to foster critical thinking.

Critical Thinking and Democratic Living. Finally, consider the relation between critical thinking and democracy. It is a truism that the properly functioning democracy requires an educated citizenry. What sort of education does such a citizenry require?

The answer is not one-dimensional. The democratic citizen requires a wide variety of the many things education can provide. She needs to be well informed with respect to all sorts of matters of fact; to fully grasp the nature of democratic society and to fully embrace its responsibilities; to treat her fellow democrats as equal partners in political life; and so on. She also needs to be able to examine public policy concerns: to judge intelligently the many issues facing her society; to challenge and seek reasons for proposed changes (and continuations) of policy; to assess such reasons fairly and impartially and put aside self-interest when it is appropriate to do so; and so on. These latter abilities are central to critical thinking. Consequently, if the democratic citizen is not a critical thinker, she is significantly hampered in her ability to contribute helpfully to public life. Democracies rely for their health and well-being on the intelligence of their citizens. My point is simply that such intelligence, if it is truly to be of benefit, must consist in part of the skills, attitudes, abilities, and traits of the critical thinker. Democracy wants not simply an intelligent citizenry, but a critical one.

Indeed, the relationship between critical thinking and democracy is a very close one. For democracy, at least ideally,

> aims so to structure the arrangements of society as to rest them ultimately upon the freely given consent of its

members. Such an aim requires the institutionalization of reasoned procedures for the critical and public review of policy; it demands that judgments of policy be viewed not as the fixed privilege of any class or elite but as the common task of all, and it requires the supplanting of arbitrary and violent alteration of policy with institutionally channeled change ordered by reasoned persuasion and informed consent [Scheffler, 1973, p. 137].

The fundamentality of reasoned procedures and critical talents and attitudes to democratic living is undeniable. Therefore, insofar as we are justifiably committed to democracy, and insofar as children have a right to participate fully in democratic life, we have yet another reason for regarding critical thinking as a fundamental educational ideal and education for critical thinking as a basic intellectual right. An education that takes as its central task the fostering of critical thinking is the education most suited for democratic life.

Critical Thinking and Indoctrination

We generally regard indoctrination as a bad thing, and an indoctrinating education as an education to be avoided. But what is so awful about indoctrination? Why should we avoid it?

These questions are insightfully considered, I think, in the context of a discussion of an intellectual right to an education for critical thinking, for an important implication of the right to an education for critical thinking is a concomitant right to avoid indoctrinative education.

There is a deep, although obvious, connection between what may be called "style of belief" and critical thinking. A person who has an evidential style of belief has a disposition to seek reasons and evidence and to believe on that basis, and this, we have seen, is a central component of critical thinking. A person with a nonevidential style of belief lacks this key feature of critical thinking. Thus far, I have offered a general defense of the ideal of critical thinking and of the child's right to become, insofar as she is able, a critical thinker. Here, I would like to say a bit more about the harm that both the ideal and the right suffer at the hands of indoctrination. Indoctrination, insofar as it is a matter of fostering a nonevidential style of belief, is fundamentally anticritical.

If I have been indoctrinated and so have developed or had fostered in me a nonevidential style of belief, I have been significantly harmed. My autonomy has been dramatically compromised, for I do not have the ability to impartially settle questions of concern to me on the basis of a reasoned consideration of the matter at hand. I am, in an important sense, the prisoner of my convictions, for I cannot decide whether my convictions ought to be what they are, and I am unable to alter them for good reasons, even if there are good reasons for altering them. Indeed, lacking the disposition to seek reasons, I am doomed to unawareness of the desirability of aligning my beliefs and actions with the weight of relevant evidence. Consequently, my life is limited. Options with respect to belief and action—and, indeed, to basic aspects of my life-style and beliefs about the worthwhile life (if I have any)—are forever closed to me, given my predisposition against the contemplation both of challenges to my unreasoned but presently held convictions and of alternatives to them. I have been trapped in a set of beliefs I can neither escape nor even question; this is how my options, and my autonomy, have been limited. I have been shackled and denied the right to determine, insofar as I am able, my own future. In being indoctrinated, I have been placed in a kind of cognitive strait-jacket, in that my cognitive movements have been severely restricted. Worse, like the typical strait-jacketed person, I have also been sedated—drugged—so that I do not even realize my plight. Such a restricted life cannot be what we desire for our children, any more than we desire it for ourselves.

The child has an overwhelming interest in avoiding indoctrination. To be so shackled, and to have her options and future so limited, is to narrow her life in a way that is as unacceptable as it is out of her control. In being indoctrinated, the child is cut off from all but a narrow band of possibilities. Her freedom and her dignity are short-circuited, her autonomy is denied, her control over her own life and her ability to contribute to community life are truncated, her mental life is impoverished. This is a description more apt of child abuse than of acceptable education. Just as we have a moral obligation to stand against child abuse, so we have a similar obligation with respect to indoctrination. Here, against the background of a comparison with critical thinking, we see what is so awful about indoctrination, and why the child should be thought of as having the right, in having the right to be a critical thinker, to avoid it.

One might think that indoctrination, even in an educational program aimed at the fostering of critical thinking, is unavoidable. Even in such a program, some beliefs must be passed along to students in the absence of rational justification, if only because students do not start life aware of the nature of reasons. It is best, however, not to regard all cases of belief inculcation without rational justification as cases of indoctrination. It must be granted that we sometimes have no alternative but to teach children, or at least to inculcate beliefs, without providing reasons that justify those beliefs. Before we can pass along reasons, the child must come to understand what a reason is. Nevertheless, we can inculcate beliefs that enhance rationality and help to develop an evidential style of belief. Such belief inculcation—even though it does not, out of necessity, include the passing on of reasons that are seen by the believer as warrant for the inculcated beliefs—ought to be considered nonindoctrinative belief inculcation.

If I get a young child to believe that the sun is ninety-three million miles from the earth, that it is better to share her toys with her friends than not to share, that 2 + 2 = 4, or that it is desirable to believe on the basis of reasons, I am not necessarily indoctrinating. I am indoctrinating only if I pass on these beliefs in such a way that the child is not encouraged to, or is prevented from, actively inquiring into their rational status—that is, if her rationality is stunted, and if she is brought to develop a nonevidential style of belief. If we inculcate beliefs without reasons but encourage the development of rationality and an evidential style of belief—that is, if we encourage the development of critical thinking—we are not indoctrinating. We cannot start out giving reasons, for the child has to learn what a reason is and what counts as a good reason—that is, the child has to learn how to evaluate reasons—before our giving reasons even makes sense (Siegel, 1980, pp. 41-42). Consequently, we have no choice but to begin by inculcating beliefs in the absence of justifying reasons, but this should not blind us to the central distinction between doing so as a necessary prelude to the development of rationality and an evidential style of belief, and doing so without regard to such further development. Only the latter is appropriately considered indoctrination. We avoid indoctrination by taking the former path: by encouraging the student to become our "critical equal" and assess for herself the strength of the support that reasons offer for inculcated beliefs; to subject reasons that we take as justificatory to her independent judgment; and to transcend her intellectual dependence on us and drive, ever more competently, her own doxastic engine. We avoid indoctrination, in short, by taking seriously—even as we inculcate beliefs, as we sometimes must, in the absence of reasons that justify those beliefs—the ideal of critical thinking and the child's right to an education for critical thinking. Thus, we need not indoctrinate students to help them become critical thinkers. We can nonindoctrinatively educate for critical thinking. Thus, we need not violate one right of the student (the right not to be indoctrinated) in order to honor another.

Critical thinking—its status as an educational ideal, and the child's right to an education aimed at fostering it—affords a fine explanation of the undesirability of indoctrinative education. Such an education flouts not only a fundamental educational ideal but also a basic intellectual right of children. In recognizing the child's right to an education that aims to foster critical thinking, we recognize the anticritical nature of indoctrination. This anticritical nature is precisely what is wrong with indoctrination and why we should avoid it.

Conclusion

I have argued that there are good reasons for thinking that children have at least one intellectual right: the right to an education aimed at the enhancement of critical thinking. The reasons offered—respect for persons, self-sufficiency and preparation for adulthood, initiation into the rational traditions, and democratic living—are diverse and wide-ranging. The implications for indoctrination are also instructive. These very different considerations all suggest not only that critical thinking is a worthy educational ideal and that the fostering of it is an important educational aim, but also that children have a right to an education that takes this aim seriously, and that we violate their right if we educate in such a way as to frustrate or fail to honor that ideal. Honoring that particular intellectual right is basic to our educational endeavors.

References

Kant, I. *Foundations of the Metaphysics of Morals.* New York: Bobbs-Merrill, 1959.
McPeck, J. E. *Critical Thinking and Education.* New York: St. Martin's Press, 1981.
Peters, R. S. "Education as Initiation" In R. D. Archambault (ed.), *Philosophical Analysis and Education.* New York: Humanities Press, 1972.
Scheffler, I. *The Language of Education.* Springfield, Ill.: Charles C. Thomas, 1960.
Scheffler, I. *Conditions of Knowledge.* Chicago: Scott Foresman and Company, 1965.
Scheffler, I. *Reason and Teaching.* New York: Bobbs-Merrill, 1973.
Scheffler, I. *Of Human Potential.* London: Routledge & Kegan Paul, 1985.
Siegel, H. "Rationality, Morality, and Rational Moral Education." *Educational Philosophy and Theory,* 1980, *12* (1), 37-47.
Siegel, H. *Educating Reason: An Essay on Rationality, Critical Thinking, and Education.* London: Routledge & Kegan Paul, in press.

Harvey Siegel is associate professor of philosophy at the University of Miami. His main interests are in philosophy of science, epistemology, and philosophy of education.

Children certainly have intellectual rights, but these are less absolute and straightforward than is commonly supposed.

Three Children's Rights Claims and Some Reservations

Colin Wringe

Someone discussing the rights of any group in an American context may derive his arguments from his country's Constitution, in the confidence that they will be taken seriously by the majority of his readers. The writer living outside that immediate tradition must start from a slightly different baseline. Like the framers of the American Constitution themselves, perhaps, he may start from the position that individuals do not enter the world in any state of servitude or subordination (Locke, [1689], 1960, p. 309), and that any just framework of freedoms, expectations, and other goods must take account of this fact.

It follows from this that individuals should be free from interference and harm and free to do as they wish (that is, possess "rights of freedom"), provided other rights are not thereby infringed. They may choose to limit their own rights of freedom by entering into obligations (Hart, 1955, pp. 175-191), which create "special rights" in others.

Arguably—and this is an aspect of the situation not emphasized by the Anglo-Saxon tradition—they are also entitled to be protected by society against certain gross harms, such as starvation and lack of elementary medical care or shelter, when they cannot provide such protection for themselves. Such a category of "welfare rights" is justified if individuals are expected to obey the laws and obligations of our society. There is no reason why people should obey laws determining the distribution of wealth, property, and other resources if those laws do not protect their most elementary needs. Children, because of their immaturity, stand in particular need of such protections.

In light of these considerations, it is proposed to examine the following intellectual-rights claims, which have from time to time been made on behalf of children: that there is a right to education; that children have a right to access to knowledge; and that children have a right to freedom of expression.

The Right to Education

Before the "deschoolers," education was generally viewed as a benefit conferred on the younger generation. Many reasons may be given for doing this. Adults may love their own children or be idealistically committed to the well-being of the world and to the younger generation in general. They may be inspired by considerations of charity and benevolence or simply aware of the extent to which their own well-being depends on the knowledge, skills, and socially acceptable behavior of the young.

To the rights advocate, such considerations are unhelpful. However imperious the obligations of charity and benevolence, they create no rights on the part of those who benefit from them, and they license no claims or complaints on the part of those who do not. If the motive is economic or otherwise prudential, there is no reason why the older generation should educate more members of the next than is necessary to ensure its own prosperity and well-being.

Olafson (1973, p. 183) attempts to counter this view by supposing that parents who bring children into the world incur an obligation to ensure that they are educated. This obligation may be seen as owed (as a special right) either to the offspring themselves, who would otherwise be exposed to the rigors of life without protection or guidance, or to society, which would have to shoulder the burden of looking after those without the necessary knowledge and skill to care for and support themselves.

The argument, however, is insufficient, for it justifies a right to education only on the part of the children of the relatively well-to-do. What is required is the justification for a universal right to education, such as that claimed in the 1948 United Nations *Universal Declaration of Human Rights* (Article 26). Such a right needs to be claimable not simply against one's parents, if such one has, but against the whole community and, if necessary, against the whole world. It is true that Olafson widens the scope of his argument by attempting to show that all who benefit from education have an obligation to contribute to the education of others, but these arguments are in themselves inconclusive (Melden, 1973, pp. 202-203) and would simply demonstrate a universal obligation of educated adults to contribute to education, rather than a universal right to receive it.

If we seek justification for a universal right to education, we are not likely to find it in the area of special rights created by the particular acts of others. Universal rights do not need to be conferred (or earned) and are of two kinds: rights to freedom, and welfare rights. The right to education is not straightforwardly a right to freedom, a right to be unhindered in one's pursuit of education by one's own efforts. More immediately promising is the possibility of regarding the right to education as a welfare right.

At an entirely primitive and elementary level, one may readily imagine the pitiful condition of someone whose physical needs were adequately met but who was denied any induction into the realms of language, conceptual understanding, knowledge of everything beyond the bounds of immediate perception, the ways of the social world, and so on. Such an elementary introduction to the ways of the world is not, perhaps, what we are normally concerned with when we claim that there is a right to education. Basic socialization at this level, it might be claimed, does not result from a positive input of effort and resources by the adult world but is simply acquired as a result of everyday interaction with adults and peers.

Nevertheless, before children enter the formal educational system, or in communities where none exists, adult members of the community (particularly mothers, no doubt) spend much time and effort teaching children to talk, answering their questions about the world, and encouraging them to join in childish and adult activities of all kinds. Even the most elementary level of induction into the ways of our society involves a positive input by adults. What is here suggested is that such activity is not merely required by the pleasures and advantages of the adults concerned; it is a right of the child, since in its total absence the child suffers a harm comparable to that suffered by individuals whom the world's social and economic arrangements deprive of other important goods.

But can the argument be extended to justify a welfare right to something more elaborate? Does it hold for a certain level of actual schooling, which takes the individual beyond an elementary introduction to the language, commonsense knowledge, and folkways of his own community and brings him into contact with a body of learning that is ultimately international?

We should, I believe, be cautious in urging that education, in this sense, is a welfare right, for the rhetoric of rights is easily abused and easily brought into disrepute. Those of us who value the benefits of formal education—science, the study of history, the arts, or whatever—may find it difficult to imagine life without them and even, in our idealistic moments, think that such a life would be in some sense less than human. Yet, however important an understanding of Archimedes' Principle, of the events surrounding the Boston Tea Party, or of the work of the French Impressionists may be to us and our way of life, it is difficult to argue that the millions who are happily ignorant of such matters suffer a deprivation comparable to a lack of the basic requirements of existence.

To neglect to send a Western child in an affluent middle-class community to school (or provide comparable experiences by other means) is to ensure that he or she will never achieve membership in his or her own or, most likely, in any other community. The same cannot be said for children of communities where education is not the norm, or where education is officially universal and compulsory but school knowledge plays little part in people's life and work. Except when lack of education, in the sense now under discussion, exposes the individual to humiliation by leaving him a simpleton or outcast in his own community, someone wishing to argue that there is a right to education must depend on other arguments.

Prime among these must be arguments to show that education is the necessary means to something else, which is itself a right. Siegel (this volume) argues that in order to exercise one's right to democratic participation, one needs to be capable of critical thinking. Other writers, taking a similar view, have placed the emphasis slightly differently. It has been held, for example (White, 1971, p. 24), that citizens of a democracy must receive at least some initiation into all the modes of understanding and evaluation available to us, since political decisions may entail the weighing against each other of a range of incommensurable considerations. Participation, even as a mere voter in a modern democracy, requires a good deal of background knowledge of just the kind that is gained in school. It is difficult to know what one would make of modern political argument without some knowledge of a geographical, historical, or mathematical kind, let alone more sophisticated studies in social, economic, or ethical fields. Such a voter would not in any true sense be casting his vote but would simply have it charmed from him by whoever presents the most pleasing appearance or most effectively appeals to his prejudices, fears, and baser instincts.

The right to democratic participation is not, of course, a mere unsupported value judgement plucked out of the air; it derives directly from the initial state of moral independence and nonsubordination to which we referred earlier. Ideally, at least, such participation provides the opportunity for all to exercise their due portion of influence on our collective undertakings. If some voters are denied the prerequisites of effective political participation, they are powerless. Their destinies are decided by others. Their interests need not be considered, for their support can always be had at less expense by the image makers and sloganeers.

The Right to Access to Knowledge

The right to access to knowledge is part of a more general right to freedom to do whatever does not itself involve any right infringement.

Normally, the rights that limit the extent of an individual's rights to freedom are the rights of others. In the case of children, however, freedom may sometimes be restricted in the interests of the child's own (welfare) right to guidance and protection. In particular, the child's right to access to knowledge may be limited on this ground.

In arguing thus, I am basically in agreement with Moshman (this volume): When adult protectiveness goes beyond what is necessary, it may constitute an infringement of the child's rights. Like Moshman, although coming to slightly different conclusions, I am essentially concerned to explore the extent to which such a limitation on the child's access to knowledge is permissible.

It is also arguable, of course, that adults may sometimes legitimately withhold knowledge from their children in the protection of their own interests or in the pursuit of aspirations of their own. The scope of this entitlement, however, is somewhat limited.

It is true that in the adult world we recognize certain rights to privacy—the right to withhold information of particular concern to oneself, which may cause embarrassment or be damaging to one's relations with others. Possibly, therefore, adults and particularly parents may legitimately withhold or discourage the seeking of information that they consider damaging to their relationships with their children. At a trivial level, this might justify some reticence in relation to sexual matters until the child is capable of some understanding of the relationship involved (and sufficiently socially advanced not to rehearse such information loudly and continuously in crowded public places). More seriously, may it not also justify temporarily drawing a veil over disreputable incidents in the family past?

Embarrassment, however, can scarcely justify more than a brief restriction of access to knowledge that is of any moment to the child— delay while a suitable occasion for a full explanation is found. As for skeletons in the family closet, if the past is truly past, perhaps it may legitimately be forgotten. But events in the family past, previous marriages, disreputable forebears, the origins of the family fortunes, and so on may often be as important to the child and his conception of himself as to the parent; unnecessarily delayed revelations may create in the child a misleading impression of his own position in the world.

A more serious question is whether adults may withhold from their children knowledge of certain aspects of reality in the interests of a given conception of family life or of bringing up one's offspring in accordance with one's own religious and philosophical convictions. Such a view is not well founded. Parents who provide the family home are no doubt entitled to some control over the ambience in which they, too, have to live. This, however, justifies placing limits on the tone and content of family conversation, rather than on what children are actually to be allowed to know. As for bringing up one's children in accordance with one's own convictions, even without the relevant legal cases discussed elsewhere in this volume it would be clear that this is a right held against the state, rather than against children themselves. It is a right to avoid indoctrination, rather than to impose it.

A parent may quite properly wish to protect his child against misleading claims, which he thinks his child is not yet sufficiently mature to criticize and reject on a rational basis. To protect someone from the inculcation of a possible falsehood, however, is not to restrict his access to knowledge; quite the reverse.

Given the same access to available information, parents are, in the long run, no more likely to come to true conclusions about the nature of the universe than their children are, so that if, by manipulating the evidence, parents were ultimately free to determine the beliefs of their children, they would sometimes be imposing on them beliefs that were false.

To claim the right to do this is grossly at variance with the essential nonsubordination and equality of individuals to each other, which operates as validly between one generation and the next as between any other groups of individuals.

Returning now to the question of restricting children's access to knowledge considered harmful to them at the current stage of their development, the extreme claim has been made (Adams, 1971, p. 87) that children have the right to totally free and unrestricted access to knowledge, "the right to learn all secrets with no holds barred." Any restriction, Adams suggests, is unnecessary and disreputable.

Yet it is not unreasonable to fear that a precocious knowledge of sexual license and perversity, of the prevalence of drug taking, and of such dishonest practices as petty theft might increase the risk of a young person's becoming involved in these activities, especially if they are widely seen as the mark of adulthood. Also, detailed and explicit knowledge of what takes place on battlefields, in slaughterhouses, operating theatres, and some kinds of brothels might at some stages be acutely distressing, not to say traumatizing.

Of course, everyone has a right to access to all such knowledge, eventually. One reason for this has already been given, and obvious disrespect is shown in supposing that others will be less capable than ourselves of coping with unpleasant facts. Furthermore, someone denied such knowledge is permanently at a disadvantage in the discussion of important matters. Such a person's contribution may always be dismissed on the grounds that he is "out of touch," unworldly, or does not know what life is about; many women have no doubt suffered this disadvantage.

This, however, does not mean that such knowledge has to be made available in an uncontrolled and indiscriminate way. The issue of the child's access to knowledge brings into question not only his right of freedom but also his welfare right to guidance and protection from harm.

The obligation this places on parents may sometimes involve constraining the child from his or her own immediate desires—as, for example, when we prevent a child from playing on the railway tracks, despite her indignant assertion that she is perfectly capable of avoiding the live rail and keeping her ear cocked for approaching trains.

The argument may be abused by overanxious parents (Holt, 1974) but this in itself does not make it invalid. The child clearly has no more interest in being corrupted or traumatized than in being run over by a train. As with other areas of freedom, the problem is to know how much and for how long one may restrict the child's freedom. Certainly, one must agree with Moshman (this volume) that childish status in itself does not imply incapacity, and that traditional views of childhood may be misleading. Empirical studies, especially those of an ethnographic kind, may show us that some children are already coping with far more knowledge than we thought possible.

Since the sole ground for restriction is the protection of young people, it follows that we are not justified in attempting to conceal certain areas of knowledge from a particular young person simply because he or she is below a certain legal age, when we know that the individual is perfectly able to take this knowledge in stride. What is perhaps less obvious is that the converse argument is equally valid. Just because the average thirteen-year-old is not harmed by confrontation with a particular area of knowledge, it does not follow that we infringe this thirteen-year-old's rights by guiding him away from topics or experiences that, as parents, we think he will still find permanently upsetting or traumatizing.

Unfortunately, this has the further consequence that the invidious task of judging the point at which a young person's knowledge is to be restricted falls to the parent or other caring adult. In this, he is not given too much guidance by generalizations about the rate at which young people develop. In this situation, one can scarcely feel that such adults should be subject to the additional onus of some kind of formal proof before they intervene. On the contrary, it would seem arguable that if we even suspect that significant harm may result from an experience or situation, it is incumbent upon us to keep the child away from that situation until we are reassured that our fears are groundless. If, at the level of physical well-being, we suspected that a playground was unsafe, we would surely be justified in preventing the child from going there, pending investigation.

Slightly different issues are raised when government, by certain legal or quasi-legal regulations, seeks to prevent young people below a certain age from obtaining certain books from public libraries, entering certain movies and other entertainments, and so on. Here, of course, the librarian or other official cannot be expected to exercise discretion in the same way as a parent would, and it is necessary to lay down some more objective guidelines.

Strictly, such guidelines do infringe the rights of those relatively mature individuals who, despite their age, would not be harmed. In the same way, laws forbidding sexual intercourse before a statutory age infringe the rights of couples ready for the experience before reaching that age, and speed limits infringe the rights of those capable of driving at higher speeds, without danger to themselves and others. This is a general feature of legal and quasi-legal situations, in which clear lines of prohibition have to be drawn in the interests of practicality. Provided great hardship is not caused, such slight infringements of the moral rights of some individuals are generally regarded as justified by the public interest (in which those individuals also share) in having rules that are easily and clearly applied. This I take to be the philosophical equivalent, as well as a useful clarification, of the "compelling reasons" argument sometimes given for limiting people's constitutional rights under certain circumstances.

In the drawing of such lines, of course, legislators must have regard for empirical information about what is or is not dangerous or harmful. To set age and other limits that are demonstrably overstringent is clearly an abuse of the rights of the whole category of individuals unnecessarily affected by them. When the avoidance of harm is concerned, however, the point at which the line is to be drawn is not the average, but rather that at which most individuals can cope without risk of harm. To let people of a certain age do something that can safely be done by the average person of that age is to expose half the age group to danger.

The Right to Freedom of Expression

In this field, the extreme position has been expressed in the claim (National Council for Civil Liberties, 1970, p. 5) that the publications of children should not be subject to "any more restriction than is suffered by other publications in society": namely, such legal restrictions as relate to libel, obscenity, confidentiality, and so on.

Claims on behalf of children to this right, as with the right considered in the previous section, often profit from the rhetoric of adult political life, in which the right to freedom of expression is considered not only a basic freedom in itself but also a necessary ingredient in democratic politics. The right to complain and criticize, it is supposed, helps to guarantee that other rights of the individual will not be abused.

At the height of the "students' rights" controversy in Britain (1968-1973), these points were vigorously made on behalf of school students when meetings and even membership in some student organizations were banned by some schools, and students were suspended or expelled for giving interviews to journalists or publishing letters and articles in the adult press or in their own magazines (Wringe, 1981, pp. 1-9). It may, however, be doubted that the relationship between children and their elders precisely parallels that between various groups of adults and the political regimes under which they live.

To begin with, children are very heavily dependent for their well-being on the efforts and goodwill of the adults around them (parents, teachers, and others). In return, it might be thought, adults have a special right to exercise some control over the public acts of the children in their charge, in order to protect rights or legitimate interests of their own. This, however, applies only when specific rights and interests of adults are involved and does not justify any blanket prohibition to publish or express opinion in general.

These points are illustrated by a consideration of possible limits to children's rights to freedom of expression in relation to censorship on grounds of morality and decency, censorship of political opinion, and limits on the criticism of particular persons and institutions.

Censorship on Grounds of Morality and Decency. Adults are legally allowed to publish a range of pornographic materials regarded as offensive by most people. They bring disrepute upon their producers and others associated with them. No one would be committing any kind of right-infringement who withdrew goodwill from someone engaged in the porn trade.

Adults cannot withdraw their goodwill from dependent children without inflicting considerable harm upon them, and a stern order to desist would seem a reasonable alternative. Parents and school alike may properly feel entitled to protect their public standing from the damage inflicted by association with youthful pornographers. The school would no doubt also point to its obligation to protect other pupils from "corruption." In any case, it is part of the duty that educators, including parents, owe the children in their charge to reprove and, if necessary, forbid what they have reason to disapprove of.

This, of course, is no more than a limiting case, for the number of active teenage pornographers (as opposed to those exploited as models by adults) is no doubt very small. Of more interest is the question raised by a sincere piece of writing, an article, a poem, or other literary piece, which might nevertheless be regarded as offensive by many adults.

If a fifteen-year-old girl were to write an unsensational, soberly presented, and factually well-documented article on teenage lesbianism, her liberal parents and coeducational day school might not be too upset. They might not even think it necessary to forbid publication or take punitive action after the event. (It is part of the hypothesis that the article is not libelous and that the writer is sufficiently mature to handle both the information involved and the experience of authorship without harm to herself.)

If, however, the writer were a pupil in a religious girls' boarding school, the school authorities would—surely with some justification—feel they had legitimate interests to defend in forbidding any such publication. So might the girl's parents if they were prominent conservatives in a devout rural community.

The point of the illustration is to distinguish between, on the one hand, the case of an adult or an institution that, in protection of legitimate interests, prevents otherwise unexceptionable freedom of expression and, on the other, a case in which a young person is more or less arbitrarily denied this freedom because an adult happens to disagree with what is written or simply because it is not the policy of the school to allow pupils to communicate with the press. Arguably, the latter case infringes the young person's rights, whereas the former does not, since his or her right of freedom is properly limited by the rights of others.

Restrictions on the Expression of Political Opinion. Arguments relating to the protection of responsible adults' reputations and associated material interests do not apply with the same force here as in the previous case. The expression of extreme or radical political views cannot be regarded as morally reprehensible, although it may be taken as a sign of foolishness or immaturity. In a democratic society, we are bound to commend rather than blame the parent who permits the expression of views with which he or she disagrees. Possibly, the adult will suffer a degree of embarrassment and perhaps some ribbing by associates. He or she may feel justified in showing anger at "being made a fool of" or even in appealing to the young person's loyalty or common sense, but it is difficult to see any case for outright prohibition.

At the height of student radicalism in the 1970s, the Monday Club (Swerling, 1972), a group of British Conservative back-bench Members of Parliament, published a document titled *Who's Getting at Our Kids?* It named, in some cases, quite eminent fathers of certain well-known student radicals. It is not known whether the fathers in question suffered any career setbacks or even any embarrassment. Presumably, this was the intention of those producing the document, but if any infringement of the fathers' rights were involved, this would seem to have been committed not by the students' expression of radical views but by the document's revelation of private family relationships.

Something may be said in defense of a school or similar institutions that forbids its students to comment on sensitive topics at times of unrest within the institution itself. When this happens, offending students may sometimes be suspended or expelled. Typically, the point is made by the school authorities, at least in Britain, that the student is not being punished for the views he holds, or even for expressing them, but for disobeying a school rule or instruction or for flouting the authority necessary to the running of any school.

No doubt, the adults involved in such incidents have become needlessly excited and have overreacted. Still, this does raise the issue of whether public expression of opinion on current issues is something that educational authorities are at liberty to forbid at will. Of course, a school is bound to do all it can to maintain the good order and harmony necessary to carry out its educational task, and some expressions of opinion may run directly counter to this. These may include extreme radical views, which depict school authority as repressive and as something to be resisted or overthrown, and provocatively racist views in schools containing more than one ethnic group. Needless to say, the proponents of both extremes are inclined to appeal to the principle of freedom of expression.

In the adult world, we condemn censorship, even when this is in the interests of good order. It is difficult to see how, to be consistent, we can forbid the expression of student opinion. The very least that would seem to be required is that there should manifestly be some "real and present danger" that the expression of certain opinions may directly lead to disorder or conflict that will be destructive of the school's educational purpose.

Limitations on the Criticism of Persons and Institutions. In a slightly different category from the foregoing are public criticisms of particular persons or institutions by their students. Of course, children have a perfect right to complain about grossly incompetent or abusing teachers, and if the normal channels for complaint are for some reason unavailable, public criticism may be the only recourse.

But without being grossly incompetent or abusing, teachers, like anyone else, may be less than perfect some of the time. The question is whether students are entitled to expose to the world their teachers' foibles, shortcomings, sundry blackboard errors, and unguarded remarks. The view that students are incompetent to judge their teachers, and therefore have no right to do so, is rejected. Childish or ignorant criticism is easily seen for what it is and ignored, and damaging personal criticism may have little to do with academic or pedagogic expertise.

The more valid argument is that teachers ought to be protected from criticism of their minor shortcomings because of the professional relationship in which they stand to their students. Teachers are unlike the politicians who voluntarily accept the hazard of criticism from opponents and from those they govern when they choose to run for office. Teachers and students are engaged in a day-to-day work relationship, which may seem to impose obligations of tolerance and discretion on both sides.

We no longer speak much of the respect that teachers are entitled to receive from their students; however, their work is arduous. They give much of themselves and may even make themselves vulnerable in their efforts to enable students to grasp new ideas and new skills. It is scarcely reasonable to expect them to do this in the presence of youngsters who are looking for ways of subjecting them to damaging, if often trivial, public criticism. To this extent, it may be thought that schools and similar institutions depend on trust and a reasonably relaxed atmosphere. (Hostile and damaging public criticisms are, of course, quite different from good-humored grousing and harmless badinage, which no reputable school or teacher would be upset by.)

Conclusion

Three children's rights claims have been examined in light of the rights of freedom, special rights, and welfare rights, derived in their turn from the consideration that individuals enter the world in a state of moral independence and nonsubordination. It has been argued that the traditional "welfare" justification of the right to education establishes no more than a right to minimal socialization and needs to be supplemented by further arguments, to the effect that education is the necessary means to other undoubted rights; and that children's rights to access to knowledge and to freedom of expression may be limited by their own "welfare" right to protection and by the special rights of others, respectively.

References

Adams, P. "The Infant, the Family, and Society." In P. Adams and others (eds.), *Children's Rights*. London: Elek, 1971.
Hart, H. L. A. "Are There Any Natural Rights?" *Philosophical Review*, 1955, *64*, 175-195.
Holt, J. *Escape from Childhood*. Harmondsworth, England: Penguin, 1974.
Locke, J. *Two Treatises on Government*. Cambridge: Cambridge University Press, 1960. (Originally published 1689.)
Melden, A. I. "Olafson on the Right to Education." In J. F. Doyle (ed.), *Educational Judgements*. London: Routledge & Kegan Paul, 1973.
National Council for Civil Liberties. *Children in School*. London: National Council for Civil Liberties, 1970.
Olafson, F. A. "Rights and Duties in Education." In J. F. Doyle (ed.), *Educational Judgements*. London: Routledge & Kegan Paul, 1973.
Swerling, S. *Who's Getting at Our Kids?* London: Monday Club, 1972.
White, P. A. "Education, Democracy and the Public Interest." *Proceedings of the Philosophy of Education Society of Great Britain*, 1971, 5 (1), 7-28.
Wringe, C. A. *Children's Rights: A Philosophical Study*. London: Routledge & Kegan Paul, 1981.

Colin Wringe studied philosophy of education at the University of London Institute of Education. He is the author of a number of books and articles on children's rights and other education topics and is currently a lecturer in education at the University of Keele.

Popular majorities often believe that their values should be taught in the schools. A paradox of educational purpose arises when liberal democratic ideals require that such values not be taught.

Populism, School Prayer, and the Courts: Confessions of an Expert Witness

Gary B. Melton

In January 1985, I received a rather frantic call from Larry Rowe, an attorney representing the West Virginia Civil Liberties Union (WVCLU) in *Walter* v. *West Virginia Board of Education* (1985; hereinafter cited as *Walter*). The WVCLU was challenging the federal constitutionality of West Virginia's newly implemented state constitutional amendment requiring public schools to set aside a brief period each day for students' "personal and private contemplation, meditation or prayer." Pursuant to the test enunciated by the Supreme Court in *Lemon* v. *Kurtzman* (1971), the WVCLU was contending that the state amendment violated the establishment clause of the First Amendment to the United States Constitution, because the new law had a religious purpose, both advanced and inhibited religion, and entangled the government with religion. A hearing was imminent on the WVCLU's motion for a preliminary injunction against enforcement of the amendment. Would I be willing, Mr. Rowe inquired, to testify as an expert—on two days' notice—on the psychological significance of the amendment? Thus began my frantic review of relevant studies and consultation with colleagues (especially David S. Hargrove and Ross A. Thompson) and an equally frenzied trip to West Virginia for several hours of testimony. This chapter is a partial chronicle of that experience and includes some thoughts it stimulated about the dilemmas inherent in teaching children about civil rights, tolerance, and respect for diverse points of view.

The Facts of the Case

West Virginia was one of twenty-five states that permitted or required a moment of silence in the public schools (*Wallace* v. *Jaffree*, 1985, opinion of J. O'Connor, concurring in the judgment, pp. 2497-2498). A few months after *Walter* was decided, the Supreme Court ruled that such state laws are unconstitutional when they are intended to promote prayer (*Wallace* v. *Jaffree*, 1985; see also *May* v. *Cooperman*, 1985). The West Virginia case was unique, however, in two ways. First, as a state constitutional amendment, the West Virginia school prayer law was the only one directly endorsed by the electorate; in fact, 80 percent of the voters had approved the amendment, a point I shall discuss later. Second, *Walter* had been argued after the law was implemented. Therefore, the WVCLU was contending that the amendment was not only facially unconstitutional but also unconstitutional as applied. Evidence was thus taken on what actually happened in West Virginia classrooms during and as a result of the period of silence.

The amendment stated that "[p]ublic schools shall provide a designated brief time at the beginning of each school day for any student desiring to exercise [the] right to personal and private contemplation, meditation or prayer. No student of a public school may be denied the right to personal and private contemplation, meditation or prayer, nor shall any student be required or encouraged to engage in any given contemplation, meditation or prayer as a part of school curriculum." The state superintendent of schools (Truby, 1984), in consultation with the state attorney general, had suggested that the "brief" exercise be neither shorter than twenty seconds nor longer than one minute. The guidelines provided that "students should be allowed to sit, stand, kneel, or engage in other acts symbolic of their faith," but that no special place should be provided for such activities and that the acts should be "done silently, without running or walking around the room." In an obvious attempt to minimize state entanglement with religion, school staff were instructed not to provide "directions on whether or how to contemplate, meditate or pray, or to whom prayer should be directed, or suggest the content of such contemplation, meditation or prayer." Instead, it was "strongly suggested" that the period of silence be introduced with only the following sentence: "A moment of silence will now be observed for contemplation, meditation, or prayer." Any questions were to evoke this terse response: "We are doing this in compliance with the state constitution." (Imagine that response to a pupil in public kindergarten!) Testimony indicated that the moment of silence was often conducted in conjunction with the pledge of allegiance; students were expected to remain standing after the pledge for the moment of silence.

The amendment had a legislative history that should have left no doubt of its intention to advance religion. References to the deity and to the need to return prayer to the public schools permeated the legislative debate on the amendment. The sponsor of the amendment, Senator Ted Stacy, publicly stated that in his opinion separation of church and state is "a myth like evolution" (*Walter*, opinion at p. 1176). Upon certifying the election results, James Manchin, then secretary of state, had announced, "This is a great day for our brothers in Christ" (*Walter*, transcript at p. 118). Interviewed by the press in the courthouse during the *Walter* hearing, Manchin indicated that he had fully intended that remark: "As a nation, one that believes in God, we should respect . . . minorities but not let them dictate to the majority what is being done. I prayed at Farmington High School and the roof didn't fall in. If I had my way, [students] would pray out loud. This is a Christian nation" (Rhody, 1985, p. 12A).

Two children testified about their experiences with the implementation of the amendment. Brent, a Catholic sixth grader, testified that he thought that if he sat during the moment of silence, his behavior would be perceived as disrespectful to the teacher and result in demerits that might prevent his going on a field trip. Sally, an eleven-year-old Jewish girl, gave testimony that was quoted at length in the opinion ultimately issued by Judge Elizabeth Hallahan (*Walter*, opinion at pp. 1170–1173). One of Sally's classmates, who had noticed her reading a book during the moment of silence, had said that she would go to hell with the other Jews. Another youngster had added that "the Jews weren't worth saving because they had killed Christ" (*Walter*, opinion at p. 1172). Sally described herself as hurt, angry, and "uncomfortable" (*Walter*, opinion at p. 1172). She also feared that if she went to the teacher, "the teacher either wouldn't listen or if the teacher did listen, there would be a big issue made out of it and I would be in the limelight for the wrong reasons and . . . I could have a lot of bad publicity" (*Walter*, opinion at p. 1173).

In addition, a rabbi testified at length about his fear that the amendment would expose Jewish children unnecessarily to anti-Semitic remarks and require them to exert "courage and determination" to avoid acting contrary to their faith (*Walter*, transcript at p. 315). One of the plaintiffs, a Jewish schoolteacher, testified that her own children feared getting into trouble at school for declining to participate in the moment of silence and that an unfair conflict had been established between "my authority in the religious sphere and the school's authority, . . . which encroached upon the religious as far as I'm concerned" (*Walter*, transcript at p. 202). She also indicated that any state involvement in religion violated the "specialness . . . of my Jewish heritage": "I was reared as a child to be very proud of my family, which had survived the Spanish Inquisition and similar sorts of issues. My children's grandparents on their father's side walked across Russia as Jewish peasants during the czarist period to escape what they felt was persecution of religion, so that religious freedom is very important in the family that I was raised in, and I have raised my children the same way" (*Walter*, transcript at pp. 201-202).

Protestant ministers who testified criticized the amendment for trivializing prayer. Teachers testified that the need to maintain silence during the mandated moment of silence, and the students' confusion about the alternatives, created new disciplinary issues and problems for teachers in remaining uninvolved in their pupils' observance of the exercise.

Psychological Issues

Although I had been solicited to testify primarily in regard to the stigmatizing effects of the amendment on children in minority religious groups, several other psychological principles raised even more substantial questions about the constitutionality of the West Virginia law. In my testimony, I noted six psychological issues.

Children's Understanding of Alternatives to Prayer. The vocabulary (for example, "contemplation") involved in the superintendent's guidelines for the conduct of the moment of silence was likely to be unfamiliar to many schoolchildren. Even without this problem, however, children in the primary and elementary grades would be unlikely to understand that they could engage in secular meditation instead of religious prayer. Just as young children tend to view moral rules in reified, concrete terms (what Piaget, 1965, termed *moral realism*), they also tend to understand theological concepts in concrete terms (see, generally, Elkind, 1970; Fowler, 1981; Goldman, 1964).

Long, Elkind, and Spilka's (1967) study of development of concepts of prayer is illustrative. At the first stage (ages five to seven), children had a vague notion of prayer in terms of ritualized versions ("Now I lay me down to sleep") and something having to do with God. In answer to a question, many children at this stage thought that animals could pray. They also tended to believe prayers to be things that somehow had to be propelled to heaven. Children at the second stage (ages seven to nine) understood prayer only in terms of the actual behaviors involved. At about age nine or ten, children began to understand prayer as a private conversation with God and to distinguish between what one thinks and what one says. Thus, children began to differentiate prayer as a covert mental activity from prayer as an overt motor activity.

It is noteworthy that Long, Elkind, and Spilka's sample was from very affluent families (mostly children attending private schools in the Denver area), and the mean ages of transition from one stage to another may have been lower than in the general population. Regardless, at least until age nine, schoolchildren are unlikely to understand the meaning of secular forms of meditation, because they cannot divorce the meaning of prayer from its concrete manifestations.

Children's Perceptions of Entitlement. On its face, the amendment at issue in *Walter* provided the right to make two choices: whether to participate at all and, if so, whether to contemplate, meditate, or pray. I have already indicated that the latter choice is probably incomprehensible to younger pupils. The former choice also is essentially meaningless to many elementary-school pupils. For a right to self-determination to be meaningful, a person must perceive the choice and understand that he or she is entitled to make it. Primary-grade and, in disadvantaged populations, intermediate-grade pupils confuse rights with those acts that authority figures permit them to exercise (Melton, 1980). Even older children and adolescents often do not understand rights as irrevocable (Grisso, 1981; Melton, 1980). Thus, many schoolchildren would be expected to be incapable of comprehending that they were entitled not to participate in the moment of silence announced by their teacher or principal.

Even if the concept were comprehensible, students might perceive that although the right not to participate was available as a matter of law, it was nonexistent as a matter of fact. Children and youth learn that fulfillment of rights is unlikely to be rewarded and may be punished. Even adolescents are apt not to exercise rights unless express approval is given for such exercise through modeling (Belter and Grisso, 1984).

Pressures to Conform. Younger pupils are unlikely to perceive significant freedom from adult influence (Fodor, 1971). A somewhat different dynamic might diminish the voluntariness of participation in middle childhood and early adolescence. Among pupils in these age groups, there is especially intense pressure to conform to peer values and behavior. In general, age is curvilinearly related to the significance of social comparisons and conformity to peers. Especially for important matters, social comparisons and peer conformity become important at about age eight and increase in significance until about age thirteen, when they begin to become less important (see Allen and Newtson, 1972; Berndt, 1983; Costanzo and Shaw, 1966; Hartup, 1970; Hoving, Hamm, and Galvin, 1969; Ruble, Boggiano, Feldman, and Loebl, 1980). Thus, for children in the intermediate and junior high grades, exercise of the right not to participate in the moment of silence (and demarcation of oneself and one's beliefs as different) may indeed require "courage and determination."

The Foot-in-the-Door Technique. Although perhaps not purposefully, school officials had made minority students' nonparticipation or unusual participation still more difficult psychologically by pairing the moment of silence with other rituals, such as the pledge of allegiance. Having already acceded to participate—indeed, take affirmative action (to stand)—for one exercise, pupils are less likely to withdraw from participation in the moment of silence (compare Saks, 1983).

Promotion of Tolerance. In the short term, the effects of the moment of silence upon children's tolerance of minority religious beliefs would be likely to depend on the means of implementation. For decades, public opinion surveys have shown the majority of Americans to favor civil liberties in the abstract but also to favor application of state power to prevent the expression of these liberties (McClosky and Brill, 1983). Socialization into a more principled mode of legal reasoning requires participation in the exercise of rights and promotion of the concept of legal continuity (understanding of the application of civil liberties in diverse, real-world, everyday contexts) (Tapp and Levine, 1974; Tapp and Melton, 1983). If the amendment operated as facially intended—if children in fact observed diverse religious expression and nonexpression in an atmosphere of tolerance—its implementation might actually have socializing effects. Children might be more likely to perceive themselves and others as entitled to exercise whatever religious faiths they had. However, achievement of such a positive result would require direct attention to helping children understand the nature of the alternatives under the amendment, the reasons for religious tolerance, and the ways it can be expressed. It is difficult to envision how such attention could be paid without entangling the public schools in religion. Certainly, the one-sentence, officially sanctioned reference to the state constitution would not help children to appreciate their own and their classmates' freedom of religion. If, in fact, children witnessed intolerance and perceived themselves as unentitled to choose whether to pray, the implementation of the amendment would be likely to have negative effects on children's legal and moral development.

Effects of Stigma. Insofar as conditions favorable for development of tolerance are not present, prejudice is apt to be expressed. Contact with minority groups is not enough to diminish prejudice; a cooperative, egalitarian climate is required (Allport, 1954; Slavin, 1985). Absent such an atmosphere, the well-documented deleterious personal and social effects of stigma are likely to apply (see, for example, Goffman, 1963). It does not take a psychologist to recognize that rejection damages self-esteem and fosters anger and depression (see Coopersmith, 1967; Rohner, 1986). Peer rejection is likely to be especially pernicious in late childhood and early adolescence, when social comparisons with peers are particularly important in self-evaluation (Ruble, Boggiano, Feldman, and Loebl, 1980). In such a context, intergroup relations are apt to become more uncomfortable and more strongly characterized by exaggerated, rigid normative behavior (Stephan and Stephan, 1985). In short, negative personal and social consequences can be expected from the sort of stigma experienced by Sally, the Jewish girl who testified, as a result of her expression of a minority response to the moment of silence.

The Holding

To the apparent surprise of the parties, Judge Elizabeth Hallahan ruled immediately at the end of the hearing in favor of the plaintiffs. A Reagan appointee, she clearly found her decision to be personally conflict-laden and politically unwise, although guided by "ample [legal] precedent" (*Walter*, opinion at p. 1173). "From a personal and moral standpoint . . . ," she wrote, "the decision herein contained is the most difficult one with which this Court has ever been faced and, indeed, is likely as exacting as any which will ever come before it" (*Walter*, opinion at p. 1173). Nonetheless, Judge Hallahan minced no words in attacking the sponsors of the amendment: "This Court cannot refrain from observing that in its opinion a hoax conceived in political expediency has been perpetrated upon those sincere citizens of West Virginia who voted for this amendment to the West Virginia Constitution in the belief that even if it violated the United States Constitution, 'majority rule' would prevail. There is no such provision in the Constitution" (*Walter*, opinion at pp. 1177–1178).

Populism and Civil Rights in Conflict

The vote on the amendment at issue in *Walter* had left no doubt about the will of the majority. If the majority had ruled, there would have been a moment of silence in West Virginia public schools every day. Furthermore, the history of the amendment had left no doubt about the expectations of the majority for whether prayer, meditation, or contemplation would be the order of the day. If the majority had ruled, there would have been a moment of prayer—Christian prayer—in West Virginia public schools every day.

In thinking about the meaning of the overwhelming vote in favor of the amendment, it is useful for us to recall other events in the debate over religion in the West Virginia schools. Notably, in protest of the adoption of supplementary "multicultural" texts in language arts by the Kanawha County school board, rural fundamentalist parents engaged in nationally publicized demonstrations, protest meetings, school boycotts, wildcat strikes, and occasional vandalism and violence in 1974 (see Billings and Goldman, 1979, 1983; Page and Clelland, 1978; Parker, 1975). The symbolism of the protest was exemplified by a demonstrator's sign that proclaimed, "Even Hillbillies Have Constitutional Rights" (Parker, 1975, p. 30). Another protester summarized the dispute as a response to "an insidious attempt to replace our periods with their question marks" (Page and Clelland, 1978, p. 276).

The larger meaning of the Kanawha County textbook dispute has been summarized as a revolt "against school authority in defense of Appalachian working-class culture, which includes Evangelical Protestantism" (Billings and Goldman, 1983, p. 80). Religious fundamentalism long has been a central value of rural poor and working-class Appalachian people (Hood, 1983), and fundamentalist churches in central Appalachia often have allied themselves with mine workers' unions and other antiestablishmentarian movements (Billings and Goldman, 1979, 1983; Gaventa, 1980). Thus, to many West Virginians, the prayer amendment probably did not represent merely an endorsement of religion or even an expression of intolerance for minority religious beliefs. Rather, it was a defense of a way of life and of the core values of an economically and politically beleaguered populace—a revolt against elite challenges to a class and a region in which religion has served as a marker of culture.

As Senator Stacy described the public reaction to the *Walter* decision, "We here in West Virginia feel very strong and people are very religious over here, and they feel . . . that their rights have been taken away, particularly for their children. And they're just mad" (Dellinger, 1985, p. A9).

The assistant attorney general who cross-examined me in the *Walter* hearing attempted (apparently unsuccessfully) to capitalize on these sentiments by painting me as an intellectual outsider. He asked a series of questions about whether I had previously conducted interviews in West Virginia, visited classrooms in West Virginia, or even visited West Virginia at all. He prefaced his cross-examination by identifying himself as "just a country lawyer from Hurricane, West Virginia" and without knowledge of psychology (*Walter*, transcript at p. 285).

Trial strategy aside, though, the surplus meaning of the amendment and the litigation it spawned suggests one of the inherent difficulties in vindicating schoolchildren's freedoms of expression and religion (compare Melton and Saks, 1985). When the majority holds antilibertarian views, promotion of libertarian values is in conflict with itself; the consent of the governed seems not to apply. By the same token, when a school board permits the expression of antilibertarian or antidemocratic views, it is tacitly inculcating antilibertarian values. Yet, if it censors those views, it also is tacitly inculcating antilibertarian values. When a school board attempts to make opportunities for religious or political expression available to students, is it promoting self-determination and socializing children to think through alternatives and make choices on their own? Or is it tacitly promoting particular perspectives? When, as in *Walter*, the attempt to assert particular values is perhaps the product of self-protection and forthright use of the democratic process by a class under siege, does the populist coloring of the antilibertarian movement change the proper response to it? Can we protect minorities' freedom of expression and still tolerate intolerance?

In short, attempts to inculcate libertarian values are apt to have at least some paradoxical effects. Efforts to promote children's intellectual, political, and religious exercise are likely to expose them to expressions of values antithetical to such exercise. When the will of the majority is itself counter to such exercise, promotion of libertarian values may seem to conflict with the exercise of political autonomy by the common person. These dilemmas complicate the already complex and difficult task of teaching children the core values of a liberal democratic society. Besides the reallocation of power necessary to provide children with actual free exercise, such a goal necessitates overcoming the confusion engendered by abstract, paradoxical concepts and by the intellectual conflicts within our political culture itself.

These dilemmas are especially profound when the majority is itself oppressed and therefore prone to respond rigidly and defensively to minority views (Katz and Glass, 1979). Few lessons are harder to learn than the principle that neither cultural values nor personal autonomy will solidify by turning "question marks" into "periods," as if one had a monopoly on the truth. Regardless, the truth surely is not so fragile that it will disintegrate in the face of expression of unpopular beliefs. The dignity both of oppressed majorities and of stigmatized minorities can be best protected by preserving zones of personal belief and expression that are invulnerable to the whims of the powerful. Tolerance of minority views ultimately also protects the majority against politically and economically powerful elites. The agenda for educators is to inculcate respect for human rights. Majority rule is an instrument of personal expression, not an end in itself.

References

Allen, V. L., and Newtson, D. "Development of Conformity and Independence." *Journal of Personality and Social Psychology*, 1972, *22*, 18-30.
Allport, G. *The Nature of Prejudice*. Cambridge, Mass.: Addison-Wesley, 1954.
Belter, R., and Grisso, T. "Children's Recognition of Rights Violations in Counseling." *Professional Psychology: Research and Practice*, 1984, *15*, 899-910.
Berndt, T. J. "Social Cognition, Social Behavior, and Children's Friendships." In E. T. Higgins, D. Ruble, and W. Hartup (eds.), *Social Cognition and Social Development: A Sociocultural Perspective*. Cambridge, England: Cambridge University Press, 1983.
Billings, D. B., and Goldman, R. "Comment on 'The Kanawha County Textbook Controversy.'" *Social Forces*, 1979, *57*, 1393-1398.
Billings, D. B., and Goldman, R. "Religion and Class Consciousness in the Kanawha County School Textbook Controversy." In A. Batteau (ed.), *Appalachia and America: Autonomy and Regional Dependence*. Lexington: University Press of Kentucky, 1983.
Coopersmith, S. *The Antecedents of Self-Esteem*. San Francisco: Freeman, 1967.
Costanzo, P. R., and Shaw, M. E. "Conformity as a Function of Age Level." *Child Development*, 1966, *37*, 967-975.
Dellinger, P. "Opponents Hope Prayer Amendment Won't Stand Up." *Roanoke Times and World News*, February 17, 1985, pp. A1, A9.
Elkind, D. "The Origins of Religion in the Child." *Review of Religious Research*, 1970, *12*, 35-42.

Fodor, E. M. "Resistance to Social Influence Among Adolescents as a Function of Moral Development." *Journal of Social Psychology*, 1971, *85*, 121–126.

Fowler, J. *Stages of Faith: The Psychology of Human Development and the Quest for Meaning*. New York: Harper & Row, 1981.

Gaventa, J. *Power and Powerlessness: Quiescence and Rebellion in an Appalachian Valley*. Urbana: University of Illinois Press, 1980.

Goffman, E. *Stigma: Notes on the Management of Spoiled Identity*. Englewood Cliffs, N.J.: Prentice-Hall, 1963.

Goldman, R. *Religious Thinking from Childhood to Adolescence*. London: Routledge & Kegan Paul, 1964.

Grisso, T. *Juveniles' Waiver of Rights: Legal and Psychological Competence*. New York: Plenum, 1981.

Hartup, W. W. "Peer Interaction and Social Organization." In P. H. Mussen (ed.), *Carmichael's Manual of Child Development* (3rd ed.). Vol. 2. New York: Wiley, 1970.

Hood, R. W., Jr. "Social Psychology and Religious Fundamentalism." In A. W. Childs and G. B. Melton (eds.), *Rural Psychology*. New York: Plenum, 1983.

Hoving, K. L., Hamm, N., and Galvin, P. "Social Influence as a Function of Stimulus Ambiguity at Three Age Levels." *Developmental Psychology*, 1969, *1*, 631–636.

Katz, I., and Glass D. G. "An Ambivalence-Amplification Theory of Behavior Toward the Stigmatized." In W. Austin and S. Worchel (eds.), *The Social Psychology of Intergroup Relations*. Monterey, Calif.: Brooks/Cole, 1979.

Lemon v. Kurtzman, 403 U.S. 602 (1971).

Long, D., Elkind, D., and Spilka, B. "The Child's Conception of Prayer." *Journal for the Scientific Study of Religion*, 1967, *6*, 101–109.

McClosky, H., and Brill, A. *Dimensions of Tolerance: What Americans Believe about Civil Liberties*. New York: Russell Sage Foundation, 1983.

May v. Cooperman, 780 F.2d 240 (3d Cir. 1985).

Melton, G. B. "Children's Concepts of Their Rights." *Journal of Clinical Child Psychology*, 1980, *9*, 186–190.

Melton, G. B., and Saks, M. J. "The Law as an Instrument of Socialization and Social Structure." In G. B. Melton (ed.), *Nebraska Symposium on Motivation*. Vol. 33. *The Law as a Behavioral Instrument*. Lincoln: University of Nebraska Press, 1985.

Page, A. L., and Clelland, D. A. "The Kanawha County Textbook Controversy: A Study of the Politics of Life Style Concern." *Social Forces*, 1978, *57*, 265–281.

Parker, F. *The Battle of the Books: Kanawha County*. Bloomington, Ind.: Phi Delta Kappa Educational Foundation, 1975.

Piaget, J. *The Moral Judgment of the Child*. New York: Free Press, 1965.

Rhody, J. P. "Superintendent: Prayer Amendment Intended to Lessen State Involvement." *The* (Beckley, W. Va.) *Register/Herald*, January 31, 1985, pp. 1A, 12A.

Rohner, R. P. *The Warmth Dimension: Foundations of Parental Acceptance-Rejection Theory*. Beverly Hills, Calif.: Sage, 1986.

Ruble, D. N., Boggiano, A. K., Feldman, N. S., and Loebl, J. H. "Developmental Analysis of the Role of Social Comparison in Self-Evaluation." *Developmental Psychology*, 1980, *16*, 105–115.

Saks, M. J. "Social Psychological Perspectives on the Problem of Consent." In G. B. Melton, G. P. Koocher, and M. J. Saks (eds.), *Children's Competence to Consent*. New York: Plenum, 1983.

Slavin, R. E. "Cooperative Learning: Applying Contact Theory in Desegregated Schools." *Journal of Social Issues*, 1985, *41* (3), 45–62.

Stephan, W. G., and Stephan, C. W. "Intergroup Anxiety." *Journal of Social Issues,* 1985, *41* (3), 157-175.

Tapp, J. L., and Levine, F. J. "Legal Socialization: Strategies for an Ethical Legality." *Stanford Law Review,* 1974, *27,* 1-72.

Tapp, J. L., and Melton, G. B. "Preparing Children for Decision Making: Implications of Legal Socialization Research." In G. B. Melton, G. P. Koocher, and M. J. Saks (eds.), *Children's Competence to Consent.* New York: Plenum, 1983.

Truby, R. "Voluntary Contemplation, Meditation or Prayer in Schools." Memorandum to county superintendents, West Virginia Department of Education, December 17, 1984.

Wallace v. Jaffree, 105 S.Ct. 2479 (1985).

Walter v. West Virginia Board of Education, 610 F. Supp. 1169 (S.D. W. Va. 1985).

Gary B. Melton is professor of psychology and law and director of the law/psychology program at the University of Nebraska-Lincoln. He is president of the Division of Child, Youth, and Family Services of the American Psychological Association (APA), associate editor of Law and Human Behavior, *and editor of the "Judicial Notebook" column in the* APA Monitor. *In 1985 he received the APA's Award for Distinguished Contribution to Psychology in the Public Interest.*

The goal of developing the intellectual capacities of children in public schools requires careful balancing of children's intellectual rights with the concerns of parents, teachers, and makers of educational policy.

Children's Intellectual Rights: Implications for Educational Policy

Bridget A. Franks

The chapters in this volume have argued from various perspectives that children possess certain intellectual rights that must be respected by the adults who care for and assume responsibility for them. Some of these rights are legally recognized by the Constitution of the United States and various state governments, while others have no legal status but can be justified on the basis of philosophical principles. Assuming children do have the right to use and develop their intellectual capacities, and assuming as well that schools have something to do with the intellectual development of children, how should schools act to protect the intellectual rights of their pupils?

While it is necessary to consider the concept of intellectual rights in the abstract, the issues become even more complex when viewed in light of the history, nature, and purpose of education. When the concept is applied to the actual educational experience of children, we must deal with a network of interrelations among children's rights, legal constraints, and the interests of people who make schools function. We must consider how children's intellectual rights can be reconciled with parental rights, teachers' academic freedom, and decisions about educational policy.

Students, parents, and educators may at times appear to be at cross-purposes with regard to educational decisions. Certainly, they tend to look at the issues from different perspectives. This chapter will examine the concept of children's intellectual rights from each of these perspectives, considering how the concept interacts with the roles, functions, and interests of each. In addition, it will provide specific guidelines for dealing with issues raised by the concept of intellectual rights in public educational settings.

Public Education

Most of the issues considered here will relate primarily to public, rather than private, schools in the United States. Public schools, as institutions of the government, have a unique role in communicating not only intellectual skills but also societal values and expectations. Moreover, because public schools are government institutions, both the Constitution and statutory laws apply to them in different ways than they do to private schools.

Further, public schools represent a concept central to the functioning of American society: equal opportunity. We take this as a given, forgetting sometimes that it has not always been the case that every child in the United States had, at least in principle, an equal opportunity for an education. But any discussion of the intellectual rights of children needs to take into account the opportunities children are likely to have to develop their intellectual capacities in an educational setting. Free public schools represent our attempt to guarantee all children, regardless of socioeconomic status, those opportunities.

An additional consideration, of course, is that education in our society is not only a right but a requirement. In making at least a minimal amount of education compulsory for all citizens, our government assumes a responsibility for providing that education to those who could not otherwise afford it. There is, after all, no point to a law that requires all children to be educated unless all children have a genuine opportunity to receive that education.

Public schools in the United States are charged with many obligations. As Siegel (this volume) notes, they must educate people to take their place in a functioning democracy. A democracy requires citizens who can vote in an informed manner, having considered the issues and made a reasoned decision about them. Schools, then, must provide opportunities for students to develop the kinds of skills they will need to be informed citizens, which implies allowing and even encouraging critical thinking and independent decision making.

But schools have other charges as well. They are expected to transmit to students such societal values as hard work, independence, and respect for the rights of others. So, in addition to fostering critical thinking, schools are also expected to do a certain amount of inculcating of their students. While these roles may seem contradictory, inculcation has a long history; as van Geel (this volume) reminds us, every Justice of the current Supreme Court has embraced the proposition that public schools may seek to inculcate pupils. Whether or not such inculcation moves into the realm of indoctrination and thus violates the intellectual rights of children (Siegel, this volume), public schools continue to face pressure to instill the values of a democratic society into their pupils.

It seems that schools must walk a fine line if they are to fulfill all their obligations. They must transmit the values and expectations of society while simultaneously facilitating children's abilities to think critically and make informed decisions. They must communicate a body of knowledge and demonstrate that pupils have learned it. Further, as the U.S. Supreme Court has indicated, they must respect the constitutional rights of the children in their charge (*Tinker* v. *Des Moines Independent Community School District*, 1969). Finally, they must respect input from parents and the academic freedom of teachers. Clearly, public schools have no easy task to accomplish.

Issues for Educators

Teachers, school administrators, and school board members all have a common interest and concern in providing for the educational needs of children. The concept of intellectual rights has a number of implications for them to consider as they go about this important work.

Public schools in the United States must serve and respect the rights of all students and must recognize and allow for the expression of a variety of different opinions and viewpoints. Just as our Constitution recognizes the pluralism of a democratic society, so must our schools. Thus, it is inevitable that children in public schools will be exposed to a variety of ideas, rather than to one particular set of values and beliefs (as may be the case in a private school). In addition, professional educators are aware of psychological research, such as the work of Piaget, which indicates that exposure to a variety of ideas facilitates the development of intellectual abilities such as critical thinking and scientific reasoning (Berkowitz and Gibbs, 1985).

Not all parents, however, share the view that children have intellectual rights and that education should foster critical thinking. To some parents, education can and should be an indoctrination of the values and attitudes held by adults. To these parents, the role of the public school is to transmit their values and discourage children from questioning them. This view poses a fundamental problem for the school administrator: Whose values should be chosen for indoctrination? Parents (and their children) possess a wide variety of values, and the public school must respect all of them equally if it is not to deny freedom of expression to some people.

As any school administrator knows, schools are both more accessible and more vulnerable to public pressure than many other civic entities. Fighting city hall can be a task fraught with red tape and other difficulties, but calling a child's principal and objecting to a textbook or to a class discussion is much more manageable. And, of course, parents are entitled to have input into decisions about their children's education. But the school's task is to accommodate parents of all inclinations and to allow for input from many viewpoints. Clearly, parents who want their children exposed to only their own views are going to be unhappy with this situation.

Public schools are increasingly under fire these days from a number of sources, often conflicting in their complaints. Controversy must be expected, and school districts would do better to anticipate it and be prepared than to wait and react after a conflict arises. It is also useful, when controversy occurs, if teachers and administrators can present a united perspective to parents. In the case of objections to textbooks or classroom activities, for example, pressure groups may target particular teachers and pit them against administrators, thus splintering the educational system and hindering resolution of the issue. If educators of all kinds can stand and work together, the delicate task of balancing parent, student, and teacher rights to free thought and expression will be much easier.

Practical Steps for Educators

1. If you are involved in making educational policies, you should be aware both of children's constitutional rights in school and of the rights of teachers in such settings. School policies relating to lesson plans, textbooks, or any other curriculum issue should reflect this awareness.

2. Your school system should have established adoption procedures, which are made clear to the public before any curriculum materials are adopted. These procedures should include a written list of criteria to be used in the selection of textbooks and other curriculum materials. While the criteria may be subject to criticism, an individual book or other resource that fits agreed-upon guidelines should not be (Parker, 1979).

3. With regard to textbook challenges, your district should have established procedures for dealing with complaints about textbooks, library books, and other materials. No item should be removed until the entire procedure has been followed (Parker, 1979). Jenkinson (1986) offers sample policies from several school districts and guidelines for implementation.

4. Investigate the source of complaints about books or attacks on teachers. Local parent groups are often backed by powerful national orga-

nizations, such as the Moral Majority, the Eagle Forum, or the Heritage Foundation. Such groups encourage the use of tactics like these, advocated by Connaught Marshner (1979, p. 191) in *Blackboard Tyranny*: "If you mean to circulate a rumor, don't do it on your official stationery or in the name of your group. . . . Make sure the targeted school board member feels your opposition. Seed the candidate's forum with hostile questions. . . . The point is not so much to change the board as it is to make a target of John Doe, thus teaching future board members a cautionary lesson. . . . Never give the appearance of being organized." Be aware that what looks like a lot of complaints may all be coming from one group. Try to discourage such counterproductive tactics as the targeting of individuals for personal, hostile attacks.

5. Finally, be aware of and use due process in academic freedom cases and other challenges to books or teaching. Uerling (1985) summarizes the basic requirements of constitutional due process in public education in two general ideas: adequate justification of governmental actions to avoid impermissible impingements on constitutionally protected personal rights; and adequate procedures to guard against mistaken or unjustified deprivations of protected interests. As he points out, "If a purpose of schooling is to inculcate an appreciation of the American system of government, then the actions of governing boards and administrators should stand as a model of sensitivity to the protected rights of employees and students."

Particular Issues for Teachers

Teachers in public schools are probably aware of recent increases in censorship in classrooms and school libraries. Now, more than ever, they may find themselves being ordered to black out words, remove lesson plans, or design alternative reading assignments for students whose parents object to certain books. They have lost their jobs for teaching banned books, using taboo words in class, teaching such unpopular subjects as sex education, or even objecting to book-banning. Some teachers have been reinstated after going to court, but others have not. Court decisions have been varied, with some based on First Amendment rights and others on procedural issues, age of pupils, and other circumstances (Hoy, 1977).

Even when teachers are successful, the financial and emotional cost of fighting censorship can be high (*Stachura* v. *Truszkowski*, 1985). Rather than dealing with reprimands, threats, or lawsuits, some teachers censor themselves. They retain their job security at the cost of their personal and professional integrity (Simmons, 1981). Others have chosen to resign rather than deal with constant censorship and harrassment ("Censorship Dateline," 1986). To avoid having to make such decisions there are several things teachers can do.

Practical Steps for Teachers

1. Work for established procedures for curriculum adoption in your school system, and for a formalized school-board policy on the teaching of controversial issues.

2. Find out about your district's procedure for handling complaints about teachers. Make sure it guarantees due process and discourages hasty administrative action (Rossi, 1982).

3. Make what efforts you can to turn censorship incidents into constructive experiences for students and parents. Teachers throughout the country have used the objections of censors as spinoffs for discussion and writing assignments. Students' responses, usually in defense of their freedom to read, have helped to relieve the tension in textbook controversies. Parents realize their children have not been corrupted, and students have a chance to exercise their reasoning abilities ("Our Readers Write . . . , 1981). In one community, teachers organized a class for parents to read and discuss controversial books used in the curriculum. Complaints were replaced with strong community support for the books and praise for the dedication of the teachers (Kamhi, 1982).

4. In acting to protect their own academic freedom, teachers incur a professional obligation to be equally sensitive to the rights of students to be exposed to a variety of viewpoints, not just those of their teachers. As the work of many psychological researchers has shown, children are more likely to accept without question the views of authority figures, such as parents and teachers, than they are to accept the views of peers (Forman and Kraker, 1985). When children passively accept solutions imposed by such authority figures, little cognitive progress is made (Mugny and Doise, 1978). In contrast, as Moshman (this volume) points out, there is a good deal of evidence that exposure to differing viewpoints and ideas promotes cognitive growth. Teachers need to consider this evidence if they are to implement Siegel's (this volume) view that students should be treated with respect.

5. If you do become involved in a censorship or other teaching controversy, keep in mind that you must follow all district procedures for handling such cases. You cannot go to court until all administrative channels have been exhausted.

6. Be aware that you cannot automatically count on your school's administrators either to know your rights or to protect you. In a study of high school principals and their knowledge about censorship issues, Anderson and Wetzel (1982) found that most of the principals polled did not have a clear understanding of legal issues involving censorship and teachers' rights, although they did know the proper legal procedures for removing teachers.

7. If you need it, legal advice is available from the National Educa-

tion Association, the American Federation of Teachers, and the American Civil Liberties Union.

8. Don't resign prematurely. You have due process rights guaranteed in the Constitution. You should not resign until all procedural alternatives have been attempted (Rossi, 1982).

Issues for Parents

The Reverend Jerry Falwell, founder of the Moral Majority, once stated, "I hope I live to see the day when, as in the early days of our country, we won't have any public schools. The churches will have taken them over again and Christians will be running them" (Hechinger, 1985). Falwell neglected to mention that in those "early days," many children (those whose parents could not afford church-run schools) had no opportunity for any sort of education, religious or otherwise. In the days before public education, not only children's education levels but also their social status and career choices were determined by those of their parents. The possibility of rising above the level of one's parents, whether educationally or in some other respect, is a consequence of a number of social changes, probably none so important as public education. Through it, all children, regardless of their parents' education, wealth, or social status, have (ideally) an equal opportunity to develop their intellectual capacities.

But education is not only available to all children in the United States; it is also required of them. Children have to attend school for a certain number of years, regardless of how parents feel about the issue. The fact that education is compulsory in America removes children, at least to some degree, from their parents' control. The issue of control over education, for parents and for the state, is important to the consideration of children's intellectual rights.

Parents have, of course, a legitimate interest in their children's education and in the kinds of intellectual experiences their children have. Public schools, as previously stated, have an obligation to serve all children and respect the viewpoints of a variety of people. Consequently, it is inevitable that children attending public schools will be exposed to opinions, values, and life-styles different from their own. In making decisions about their children's education, parents need to recognize which elements they can control and which they cannot. They cannot, for example, decide that their children will remain uneducated for life. They can, however, decide where to send their children to school or whether (within certain restrictions) to educate them at home. If they decide to send their children to public schools, they need to recognize the pluralistic nature of such institutions.

Schools in America have come increasingly under attack, for all kinds of reasons. Blamed by one voice or another for every social ill that besets the nation, they find themselves pressed from many sides to fulfill a varied agenda. Many parents feel it is important for schools to transmit the parents' own moral values or at least to refrain from teaching ideas inconsistent with them. They feel that exposure to values different from their own may hinder or undermine the moral training given to children by their parents. The problem with this, of course, is that practically any idea can be inconsistent with someone's moral or religious values. The inevitable conflicts raised by this situation are exemplified by a recent campaign of actions related to the 1978 Hatch Amendment.

In 1978, Senator Orrin Hatch (R-Utah) amended the General Education Provisions with what has since been called the "child privacy act." The new federal law prohibited the use of psychiatric examination, testing, or treatment of students without parental approval. It also required school systems to provide a procedure to hear and act on parental complaints about such psychiatric treatment or testing.

In writing the regulations used to implement the new law, the Department of Education (DOE) was heavily influenced by Phyllis Schlafly and the Eagle Forum. Over the vigorous objections of many educational organizations, regulations were adopted that expand the enforcement of the Hatch Amendment well beyond complaints about psychiatric testing or treatment. Under the new regulations, published in the fall of 1984, the amendment now covers classroom teachers, teaching methods, and classroom materials. If a parent objects to what or how a teacher in a particular district is teaching, it is possible to initiate a federal investigation that could result in loss of federal funding for the school district (Krug, 1985).

Since the publication of the new regulations, numerous complaints (mostly in form letters provided by groups such as Schlafly's) have been made to school districts in at least seventeen states (Jenkinson, 1986). The letters ask that school districts seek written parental permission before raising for classroom discussion any of a large number of topics, ranging from alcohol and drugs to nuclear war. While the regulations say that parents must attempt to resolve their complaints at the local level, there is no requirement that local remedies be exhausted, but only that there be an attempt to resolve the problem locally before involving the U.S. Department of Education. There are no provisions for procedures at any complaint level, and there is no court of appeals for those who might disagree with the Department of Education's decision. Some schools have reacted by forbidding teachers to mention certain controversial topics in the classroom (Krug, 1985).

The controversy over the Hatch Amendment will no doubt continue for some time. Hatch himself has renounced the broad interpretation of the DOE regulations, stating his amazement at such misinterpretation of the Hatch Amendment (Krug, 1985). Efforts are currently being made by educational groups to persuade the Department of Education to withdraw or revise the regulations and to develop legislation that will overturn the effects of the rules. The DOE, for its part, has assured at least one school district (Merrick, New York) that it will not intrude in any local program or activity. The Hatch regulations, it stated, concern only procedures for parental notification and any subsequent complaint ("Scratch Hatch," 1986).

Whatever eventually happens with the Hatch Amendment, schools and parents alike need to consider what constitutes appropriate parental intervention in teaching and program planning in public schools. How can schools respond to legitimate parental concerns about what children are learning and still respect the differing views of all? Some Religious Right organizations have made very clear their intention to transform the country's public education system, according to their own moral beliefs and regardless of the concerns of other people who use the schools. But censorship attempts have been made in schools by people representing a variety of perspectives, not just those of the Right (Jenkinson, 1986). How can parents deal with issues of control over what children learn in public schools?

One important decision parents need to make has to do with the amount of exposure children will have to ideas and values different from their own. If parents feel strongly that such exposure is damaging to their children, they need to recognize that it is inevitable in public schools, where—no matter what the lesson plans are—the children themselves will have differing perspectives. If parents want total control over the ideas their children are exposed to, they may want to consider private education. But it is important to realize that no matter what children see, hear, and are exposed to, they invariably think for themselves, to some degree. It is impossible to control every thought another person has, no matter how strictly an educational or moral treatment is applied. Sooner or later, most children will begin to think for themselves and to question the values and beliefs of their parents; this is part of becoming an adult.

Consideration of this natural developmental process may make it easier for parents to deal with children's questioning when it occurs. It may also help parents to know that research in developmental psychology has long recognized the utility of exposure to differing opinions, especially from peers, for mature cognitive and social development (Berkowitz, 1985). In addition, studies have shown that children from families that resolve conflict through fair, open discussion reason at higher stages of moral development than those who have not had this kind of experience (Parikh, 1980; Stanley, 1980). Involving children in discussions about morals and values can be a way of ensuring that those values are thoroughly understood and deeply explored, rather than unthinkingly accepted.

Practical Steps for Parents

1. Be aware of your school district's policies for dealing with controversies, and insist that they be followed. If the policies are inadequate or unfair, work to revise them.

2. Let your voice be heard, and be tolerant of the voices of other parents as well. If something you like is happening in your child's school, be vocal in your support. Let the school know when you approve as well as when you disapprove.

3. Support your children's right to explore new ideas and be exposed to different viewpoints. Work against the restriction of controversial books and ideas in school. Other parents may censor what their own children read; they should not be allowed to decide what your children may read.

4. If you decide to work actively against movements to censor or control schools, be prepared for some personal consequences. Parents involved in textbook and curriculum controversies have reported hate letters, threatening phone calls, damaged friendships, and unwanted notoriety.

5. If you are working with a national group in organizing a protest effort, keep in mind the goal and agenda of that group. National concerns of such a group may or may not reflect the local issues you are concerned about, and national groups have been known to manipulate parents' legitimate concerns about schools to achieve their own ends. Be sure you are working on the issues that really concern you and your own community.

Issues for Students

Many educational issues involve conflicts among the rights of parents, the interests of the state, and the needs of children (Moshman, 1985). When this happens, it becomes necessary for the parties involved to make compromises and work out their differences in ways that involve the least possible restriction on individual rights. In controversies between public schools and parents or between private schools and the state, the views of students themselves are often not considered. In *Wisconsin v. Yoder* (1972), for example, only the students who agreed with their parents' beliefs were allowed to testify. In the Faith Christian case in Nebraska (Moshman, 1985), no children were ever asked for comment about their educational needs and preferences.

Yet students are often aware, involved, and deeply affected by controversies in their schools. For example, students brought suit in Warsaw, Indiana, after books and courses were removed from the high school curriculum. Steven Pico and four other students challenged the removal of books from their school library in a case eventually decided by the Supreme Court (*Board of Education, Island Trees Union Free School District v. Pico*, 1982).

In *Fraser v. Bethel School District* (1985), a high school student brought a civil rights action against his school district when it suspended him for three days for his use of sexual innuendo in a nominating speech for a student candidate. The student, Matthew Fraser, was also removed from consideration to be a commencement speaker for his graduation. Both a district court and a court of appeals decided in favor of the student, holding that the school district failed to show that Fraser's use of sexual innuendo substantially disrupted the educational process and that, therefore, the district violated Fraser's constitutional right to freedom of speech when it disciplined him. In their appeals, school officials argued that schools should have a right to control "offensive" speech of students when it takes place at school-sponsored activities. In July, 1986, the Supreme Court overturned the lower courts' decisions and ruled that, at least in a public school context, the need to teach "the habits and manners of civility" takes precedence over freedom of speech (*Bethel School District* v. *Fraser*, 1986). As this case illustrates, schools do not always see students as having the same constitutional rights as adults. Nor do the courts always agree about the limits on freedom of expression for students. Students need to be aware of and sometimes fight for their rights, as they cannot always count on adults to look out for their interests.

Whether or not such a conflict is decided in court, the learning experiences of students can be seriously affected by conflicts between parents and school officials or teachers. Both groups are seen as authority figures, and it can be upsetting for students to see these figures in conflict with each other. It can also be distracting and have a negative effect on the learning environment (Nelkin, 1978). High school students in Warsaw, Indiana, reported continuing censorship of yearbook production and reading materials in 1977 and 1978. In the process of a censorship controversy, in which a number of teachers lost their jobs, the school newspaper was shut down and students' lockers were searched by police dogs. The students were troubled by the atmosphere of paranoia in which their teachers worked, and one commented, "It is too bad they're so scared they can't let their talents out" (Arons, 1979).

Students in Warsaw also reported that they had never discussed the First Amendment, civil liberties in America, McCarthyism, or the red scares of the 1920s in any history class. This kind of situation exemplifies the difficulties faced by students when their intellectual rights are not considered. Not only may they have to learn in a tense, fearful atmosphere; they may also actually be denied the opportunity to learn about their rights as American citizens, as well as about the events in history that have threatened those rights. It is asking a lot of students to expect them eventually to be responsible, informed adult citizens, when they are denied in their youth the experiences that would help them develop the skills needed for citizenship. How can students protect their own intellectual rights in educational controversies?

Practical Steps for Students

1. If you care about protecting your rights in school, you need to know what those rights are. If your school does not provide this information, the American Civil Liberties Union can be a helpful source. Two

ACLU handbooks, *The Rights of Students* (Levine and Cary, 1977) and *The Rights of Young People* (Guggenheim and Sussman, 1985), discuss freedom of expression and other civil-liberties issues. Should it become necessary, legal help is also available from the ACLU.

2. Communicate your concerns to your parents. Parents can have a lot of influence in schools; let them know their involvement is important to you.

3. Express your ideas in school. If you disagree with a teacher's views, add your own to the discussion, but don't try to suppress teachers by "reporting" their views to the administration. Respect your teachers' freedom of speech as well as your own. The same applies to other students, of course. Peer pressure can be a powerful silencer; try not to use it to squelch ideas you dislike.

4. Involve yourself in issues that concern you at school. Let the PTA, the administration, and other students know your feelings. It is your education; you have both reason and right to take an active part in it.

Conclusion

The concept of children's intellectual rights, a complex one to begin with, becomes even more complex in its application to the everyday world of the American public school. The differing views and interests of students, parents, and educators interact in ways not easy to predict. Compromises are sometimes necessary. In the pluralistic world of public education, no one is likely to be completely satisfied. But when conflicts arise and decisions must be made, keeping the concept of intellectual rights foremost in mind will be helpful. It reminds us all that the fundamental purpose of education is neither indoctrination nor inculcation, but the development of the intellect.

References

Anderson, P., and Wetzel, K. "A Survey of Legal Knowledge of High School Principals on Censorship Issues." *English Journal*, Feb. 1982, pp. 34-39.

Arons, S. "Book Burning in the Heartland." *Saturday Review*, July 21, 1979, pp. 24-29.

Berkowitz, M. W. (ed.), *Peer Conflict and Psychological Growth*. New Directions for Child Development, no. 29. San Francisco: Jossey-Bass, 1985.

Berkowitz, M. W., and Gibbs, J. C. "The Process of Moral Conflict Resolution and Moral Development." In M. W. Berkowitz (ed.), *Peer Conflict and Psychological Growth*. New Directions for Child Development, no. 29. San Francisco: Jossey-Bass, 1985.

Bethel School District v. Fraser, U.S. Supreme Court case no. 84-1667 (1986).

Board of Education, Island Trees Union Free School District v. Pico, 457 U.S. 853, 864, 102 S.Ct. 2799, 75 L.Ed.2d 435 (1982).

"Censorship Dateline." *Newsletter on Intellectual Freedom*, Jan. 1986, p. 13.

Forman, E. A., and Kraker, M. J. "The Social Origins of Logic: The Contributions of Piaget and Vygotsky." In M. W. Berkowitz (ed.), *Peer Conflict and Psychological Growth*. New Directions for Child Development, no. 29. San Francisco: Jossey-Bass, 1985.

Fraser v. Bethel School District No. 403, 755 F.2d 1356 (9th Cir. 1985).

Guggenheim, M., and Sussman, A. *The Rights of Young People*. New York: Bantam, 1985.

Hechinger, F. M. "Religion as Issue in Schools." *New York Times*, Aug. 20, 1985.

Hoy, A. K., "Controversial English Lessons and the Law." *English Journal*, Feb. 1977, pp. 21-25.

Jenkinson, E. B. *The Schoolbook Protest Movement: Forty Questions and Answers*. Bloomington, Ind.: Phi Delta Kappa Educational Foundation, 1986.

Kamhi, M. M. "Building Bridges Instead of Walls: An Anti-Censorship Effort That Worked." *Education Week*, Sept. 1982, p. 20.

Krug, J. F., "Schlafly Urges Parents to Control Teaching of Sensitive Topics." Memorandum, American Library Association, Office for Intellectual Freedom. March, 1985, pp. 1-3.

Levine, A. H., and Cary, E. *The Rights of Students*. New York: Avon, 1977.

Marshner, C. *Blackboard Tyranny*. Westport, Conn.: Arlington House, 1979.

Moshman, D. "Faith Christian v. Nebraska: Parent, Child, and Community Rights in the Educational Arena." *Teachers College Record*, 1985, *86*, 553-571.

Mugny, G., and Doise, W. "Sociocognitive Conflict and Structuration of Individual and Collective Performances." *European Journal of Social Psychology*, 1978, *8*, 181-192.

Nelkin, D. *Science Textbook Controversies and the Politics of Equal Time*. Cambridge, Mass.: MIT Press, 1978.

"Our Readers Write: How I Turned a Censorship Problem into Something Positive." *English Journal*, Dec. 1981, pp. 44-48.

Parikh, B. "Development of Moral Judgment and Its Relation to Family Environmental Factors in Indian and American Families." *Child Development*, 1980, *51* (4), 1030-1039.

Parker, B. "Your Schools May Be the Next Battlefield in the Crusade Against 'Improper' Textbooks." *American School Board Journal*, June 1979, pp. 21-28.

Rossi, J. "What Social Studies Teachers Can Do to Protect Their Academic Freedoms." *Social Education*, 1982, *46*, 276.

"Scratch Hatch." *Censorship News*, Winter 1986, pp. 2-3.

Simmons, J. S. "Proactive Censorship: The New Wave." *English Journal*, Dec. 1981, pp. 18-20.

Stachura v. Truszkowski, 763 F.2d 211 (6th Cir. 1985).

Stanley, S. "The Family and Moral Education." In R. L. Mosher (ed.), *Moral Education: A First Generation of Research and Development*. New York: Praeger, 1980.

Tinker v. Des Moines Independent Community School District, 393 U.S. 503 (1969).

Uerling, D. F. "Constitutional Due Process and Educational Administration." *ERS Spectrum*, Summer 1985, pp. 41-46.

Wisconsin v. Yoder, 406 U.S. 205 (1972).

Bridget A. Franks is a certified school psychologist and a doctoral student in developmental psychology at the University of Nebraska-Lincoln.

Index

A

Access of knowledge, children's right to, 54-58
Adams, P., 56, 62
Administrators. *See* Public schools
Allen, V. L., 67, 71
Allport, G., 68, 71
Ambach v. *Nowick*, 11, 16, 21
American Civil Liberties Union (ACLU), 81, 85
American Communications Association v. *Douds*, 12, 21
American Federation of Teachers, 81
Anderson, P., 80, 86
Arons, S., 36, 38, 85, 86
Asymmetrical Model: "agnostic" position of, 21; constitutional interpretation of, 20-21; defined, 9

B

Bearison, D. J., 32, 38
Belotti v. *Baird*, 15, 21
Belter, R., 67, 71
Bennett, W. J., 21, 22
Berkowitz, M. W., 38, 77, 83, 86
Bethel School District v. *Fraser*, 85, 86
Bickel, A., 18, 21
Bill of Rights. *See* First Amendment
Billings, D. B., 69, 70, 71
Blum v. *Yaretsky*, 15, 21
Board of Education, Island Trees Union Free School District v. *Pico*, 11, 16, 21, 84, 86
Boggiano, A. K., 67, 68, 72
Branti v. *Finkel*, 12, 22
Brendt, T. J., 67, 71
Brill, A., 68, 72
Brown v. *Board of Education*, 18, 22

C

Cary, E., 86, 87
Censorship: costs of, 79; issues, 59-60; and parents, 83-84; and teachers, 80; working with, 80

Child privacy act. *See* General Education Provisions
Child-parent-state relationship models, 8-21
Children: critical thinking of, 41-60; First Amendment rights of, 26-37; government protection of, 32-33; intellectual rights of, 26-31, 43-44, 52-62, 76-86; moral rights of, 33-35; as persons, 31-32; principles of rights of, 26-31; protection of, from parents, 15-16; psychological development of, 76, 83
Clelland, D. A., 69, 72
Constitution. *See* U.S. Constitution
Coopersmith, S., 68, 71
Costanzo, P. R., 67, 71
Critical manner, 40-41
Critical spirit, 40-41
Critical thinking: children and, 39-48, 41-60; and democratic participation, 45-46, 54, 76; education in, 40-42; as intellectual right, 40-47; style of belief and, 46
Crowley, C., 39n
Curriculum. *See* Public schools

D

Dellinger, P., 70, 71
Department of Education. *See* U.S. Department of Education, 82-83
Doise, W., 80, 87

E

Eagle Forum, 35, 79, 82
Education: for adulthood, 43-45; for critical thinking, 40-42; current issues in, 35-37; to empower students, 43-44; equal opportunity for, 76; in evolution, 36; government regulation of, 36; in human traditions, 44; legal access of, 35; moral requirements of, 43-44; nature of, 28; parents and, 81; right to, 52-54; value neutrality of, 36

Educators: issues for, 77-78; practical steps for, 78-79. *See also* Teachers
Elkind, D., 66, 71, 72
Elrod v. *Burns*, 12, 22
Emerson, T. I., 12, 22
Empowerment. *See* Education
Equal Access Act of 1984, 35

F

Faith Christian case, Nebraska, 84
Falwell, Reverend Jerry, 38, 81
Feinberg, J., 8, 11, 15, 22
Feldman, N. S., 67, 68, 72
Filardo, E. K., 32, 38
First Amendment: and children's intellectual rights, 25-38; Bill of Rights of, 31, 33; broad construction of, 26-37; establishment clause of, 63; extension of, rights, 25; intention of, 31; literal language of, 31; parents' rights and, 10; rights guaranteed by, 26-33, 37
Fishkin, J. S., 22
Fithian, L. A., 17, 22
Flagg Bros. Inc. v. *Brooks*, 15, 22
Fodor, E. M., 67, 72
Forman, E. A., 80, 87
Fourteenth Amendment, as extension of First Amendment, 25, 31
Fowler, J., 66, 72
Franks, B., 4, 25n, 75, 87
Fraser v. *Bethel School District No. 403*, 84, 87
Freedom of expression: children's right to, 58-62; restrictions on, 60-62

G

Galvin, P., 67, 72
Garvey, J. H., 20, 22
Gaventa, J., 70, 72
General Education Provisions, 82
Gibbs, J. C., 77, 86
Glass, D. G., 70, 72
Goffman, E., 68, 72
Goldman, R., 66, 69, 70, 71, 72
Government: constitutional requirements on, 34-35; restriction of children, 33, 54
Grisso, T., 67, 71, 72

Guggenheim, M., 86, 87
Gutman, A., 15, 22

H

Hamm, N., 67, 72
Hart, H. L. A., 51, 62
Hartup, W. W., 67, 72
Hatch Amendment of 1978, 82-83
Hechinger, F. M., 81, 87
Heritage Foundation, 79
Holt, J., 57, 62
Hood, R. W., Jr., 70, 72
Hoving, K. L., 67, 72
Hoy, A. K., 79, 87

I

Immigration and Naturalization Service, 17
In re Polovchak, 17, 22
Inculcation: critical thinking and, 46-48; governmental, 29-30; versus indoctrination, 29; of beliefs, 47; principle of, 29-30; of religion, 37; of values, 11. *See also* Indoctrination
Indoctrination: children's protection against, 14; and democratic theory, 13; versus inculcation, 29. *See also* Inculcation

J

Jackson v. *Metropolitan Edison Co.*, 15, 22
Jenkinson, E. B., 32, 38, 78, 82, 83, 87
Johnson, D. W., 32, 38
Johnson, R., 32, 38

K

Kamhi, M. M., 80, 87
Kanawha County school board, 69
Kant, I., 41, 49
Katz, I., 70, 72
Keyishian v. *Board of Regents*, 12, 22
Kraker, M. J., 80, 87
Kronman, A. T., 18, 19, 22
Krug, J. F., 82, 87

L

Lemon v. *Kurtzman*, 63, 72
Levine, A. H., 86, 87

Levine, F. J., 68, 73
Locke, J., 51, 62
Loebl, J. H., 67, 68, 72
Long, D., 66, 72

M

McClosky, H., 68, 72
McLaughlin, T. H., 8, 22
McPeck, J. E., 44, 49
Magzamen, S., 32, 38
March v. Alabama, 14, 22
Marshner, C., 79, 87
May v. Cooperman, 64, 72
Melden, A. I., 52, 62
Melton, G. B., 4, 63, 67, 68, 70, 72, 73
Meyer v. Nebraska, 10, 11, 22
Monday Club, 60
Moral Majority, 35, 79, 81
Moral realism, 66
Morality. *See* Education
Morris, B., 25n
Moshman, D., 4, 25, 32, 36, 38, 39n, 84, 87
Mugny, G., 80, 87

N

Narveson, B., 25n
National Council for Civil Liberties, 58, 62
National Education Association, 80-81
Nelkin, D., 85, 87
Newman, J., 25n
Newtson, D., 67, 71
Nixon v. Condon, 14, 22
Nonevidential style of belief, 46

O

Olafson, F. A., 15, 22, 52, 62
Open Future Model: aim of, 8; arguments against, 13; arguments for, 13-17; children's protection under, 15; and Constitution, 12-17; constitutional interpretation of, 18-19; and First Amendment freedoms, 12-13; implications of, 16-17; legislative regulation and, 20-21; relation to democratic theory, 13; state actor argument for, 13-14; versions of, 8-9
Orwell, G., 12, 22

P

Page, A. L., 69, 72
Parents: attitudes about education, 77-78; authority of, 10; intervention of, in schools, 82-83; issues for, 81-83; practical steps for, 83-84; rights over children, 15; withholding of knowledge by, 55-56
Parham v. J. R., 10, 22
Parikh, B., 83, 87
Parker, B., 78, 87
Parker, F., 69, 72
Peters, R. S., 44, 49
Piaget, J., 66, 72
Pierce v. Society of Sisters, 8, 15, 22
Platonic Model: central question of, 11; differences from Traditional Model, 11; versions of, 8
Plyler v. Doe, 11, 22
Poe v. Ullman, 18, 22
Polovchak v. Landon, 17, 22
Populism, and civil rights, 69-71
Prayer in schools. *See* Public schools, prayer in
Public schools: administrators in, 77-78; attack of, 81-87; and censorship, 35; controversy in, 78; curriculum and textbooks of, 78-79; inculcation of, values in students, 13, 77; obligations of, 76; parents' power over, 82; prayer in, 36-37, 63-71; task of, 77

R

Respect: as Kantian concept, 41-42; for others, 41-42
Reynolds v. United States, 12, 22
Rhody, J. P., 65, 72
Richards, D. A. J., 8, 18, 22
Rohner, R. P., 68, 72
Rossi, J., 80, 81, 87
Ruble, D. N., 67, 68, 72
Runyon v. McCrary, 22

S

Saks, M. J., 68, 70, 72
Scales v. United States, 12, 22
Scalora, M., 25n
Scheffler, I., 41, 43, 44, 45, 46, 49

Secular humanists, 36
Self-determination: of belief, 12; capacity for political, 15; children's, 16; constitutional support for, 12, 17; parents' interference with children's, 13-14, 55-56; right to, 16, 67
Self-sufficiency: and critical thinking, 44; education for, 43-45
Shaw, M. E., 67, 71
Shelly v. Kramer, 14, 22
Sher, G., 21, 22
Sherbert v. Verner, 12, 22
Siegel, H., 3, 39, 39n, 48, 49
Simmons, J. S., 79, 87
Slavin, R. E., 68, 72
Spilka, B., 66, 72
Stachura v. Truszkowski, 79, 87
Stanley, S., 83, 87
State v. Eddington, 17, 22
Stephan, C. W., 68, 73
Stephan, W. G., 68, 73
Students' rights controversy, Britain, 58
Students: empowerment of, 43-44; issues for, 84-85; moral obligations to, 40; as persons, 40-43; practical steps for, 85-86; respect for, 42; rights of, 85-86; and school controversies, 84
Supreme Court. *See* U.S. Supreme Court
Sussman, A., 86, 87
Swerling, S., 60, 62

T

Tapp, J. L., 68, 73
Teachers: and academic freedom, 80; goal of, 77; issues for, 79; moral obligation of, 42; practical steps for, 80-81; respect of, for students, 42
Teaching: critical manner of, 41-42; moral reasons for, 42-43; noninculcative, 29. *See also* Education
Terry v. Adams, 14, 22
Tinker v. Des Moines Independent Community School District, 37, 38, 77, 87

Traditional Model: authority of, 8, 10; consequences of, 8; constitutional interpretation of, 17-18; Supreme Court support of, 10-11; traditions of, 7-8
Tribe, L., 16, 22
Truby, R., 64, 73

U

U.S. Constitution: Asymmetrical Model interpretation of, 20-21; Open Future Model interpretation of, 20-21; Supreme Court's interpretation of, 7
U.S. Department of Education (DOE), 82-83
U.S. Supreme Court: rulings on freedom of speech, 85; support for Open Future Model, 12-15; support for parents and schools, 10-11
Uerling, D. F., 79, 87
United Nations *Universal Declaration of Human Rights,* 52

V

Value neutrality. *See* Education
van Geel, T., 3, 7, 22, 23

W

Walker, L. J., 32, 38
Wallace v. Jaffree, 12, 23, 64, 73
Walter v. West Virginia Board of Education, 63-66, 69, 70, 73
West Virginia Civil Liberties Union (WVCLU), 63
West Virginia school prayer law, 63-70
West Virginia State Board of Education v. Barnette, 12, 23
Wetzel, K., 80, 86
White, P. A., 54, 62
Wisconsin v. Yoder, 10, 16, 23, 84, 87
Wringe, C. A., 4, 51, 58, 62

Y

Yates v. United States, 10, 11, 23

Ministry of Education, Ontario
Information Centre, 14th Floor,
Mowat Block, Queen's Park,
Toronto, Ont.   M7A 1L2